SIGNS & SYMBOLS OF THE SUN

OTHER CLARION BOOKS
BY ELIZABETH S. HELFMAN

Maypoles and Wood Demons:
the Meaning of Trees

The Bushmen and Their Stories

Celebrating Nature:
Rites and Ceremonies Around the World

SIGNS & SYMBOLS OF THE SUN

by Elizabeth S. Helfman

A Clarion Book · THE SEABURY PRESS · NEW YORK

Acknowledgment

The extract from Akhenaten's "Hymn to the Sun"
in chapter II is from Man and the Sun *by Jacquetta Hawkes,*
copyright © 1962 by Jacquetta Hawkes,
and reprinted by permission of Random House, Inc.

Copyright © 1974 by Elizabeth S. Helfman
Book design and drawings by Ragna Tischler Goddard
Printed in the United States of America

Library of Congress Cataloging in Publication Data

Helfman, Elizabeth S.
  Signs and symbols of the sun.

  SUMMARY: Explores man's symbolic and mythical
representation of the sun in art, crafts, literature,
and religion from prehistory to the present day.
  Bibliography.
  1. Sun lore—Juvenile literature. 2. Sun-worship—
Juvenile literature. [1. Sun lore] I. Title.
BL325.S8H44   398′.362   73–20121
ISBN 0–8164–3122–1

For Paul and Helene

*"Truly the light is sweet, and a pleasant thing
it is for the eyes to behold the sun."*

ECCLESIASTES

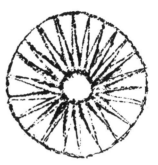

CONTENTS

I. THE SYMBOLIC SUN

Long ago in Africa a hunter painted a cross with a circle around it on a rock.

Scholars call such a design a sun wheel. It was probably a representation of the hunter's feeling about the sun that brought light to his world.

Much the same designs were made by people throughout the world; they have been found in practically every culture. This design is a symbol —a sign used to make visible what otherwise cannot be seen. Often a symbol represents an idea or a feeling that people cannot put into words.

The circle with a cross inside it was not identical everywhere. This design was found in many places, but especially in the Far East and in northern Europe. Sometimes it was turned sideways.

A sun wheel with six spokes was known to many ancient peoples. The Germanic people of northern Europe sometimes gave their sun wheel eight spokes.

Still another variation of the circle with a cross inside it is the swastika. The circle was broken and the outside lines were straightened, as you can see in the drawings.

The swastika was a well-known symbol in many countries of ancient times, from western Europe to India and China. People then believed that the sun traveled around the earth. The swastika was probably an attempt to portray the sun's motion. Each arm in the symbol represented a position of the sun on its daily journey. The arms of some swastikas pointed in a clockwise direction, as above. Others, however, turned counterclockwise.

As the sun brought life and light to the earth, so it was thought that the swastika would bring light to people, and with it joy and good health. The symbol appeared on coins and ornaments, on paintings, and on pottery. A sun disk or circle often appeared along with the swastika. Sometimes the swastika was shown inside a disk, or there might be a disk in the center of a swastika. There was even a three-legged version of the swastika that appeared on some coins in ancient times.

In the Old Testament we read that the prophet Ezekiel had a vision of four wheels, blue-green as the color of beryl stone, wheel within wheel. These, too, were probably sun wheels.

The sun itself is more than a symbol. It brings the light by which we see our world. Without the sun the earth would be dark and cold and without life of any kind.

As the sun rises in the east each day, dawn comes to first one part of the world and then another. The varied patterns of life that belong to daytime come alive. Birds begin to sing. Flowers open their petals. Many animals stir from sleep and start their day-long search for food. Most people are still asleep at dawn, but soon they, too, will be up and about their daily business.

At last, after the many hours of daylight, the sun sets in the west and night comes, as the dawn came, first to one part of the world and then to another.

Day and night make one sun pattern. The seasons make another. Long days of summer, with the sun high in the sky, bring warmth that ripens the fruits and the grain. In autumn comes the harvest. This is followed by the shorter days of winter; in the colder parts of the world everything that grows in the earth appears to die. To early people this brought fear and wondering. Would the earth ever be alive again? When the days did grow longer and spring came, people celebrated with song and dance.

The never-ending patterns of day and night, of hot summer sun, cold winter, and joyous springtime were recorded in people's minds and would remain there forever. They were as much a part of a person as sleeping and waking, eating and drinking. The bright sun became a symbol to people of all the light and growth in the world outside and within themselves.

This sun that brought so much joy could cause ruin and hardship also. The grain and the fruits of the earth might dry up under the hot sun of summer if there was too little rain. Deserts were scorched by the sun almost all the year, making life in them difficult if not impossible. Pests and diseases thrived in the fierce heat of the tropics. But even where people feared or suffered from the sun, they could not help but respect its power.

As people of ancient times watched the sun go up the sky each day, it must have seemed a miracle that only a god could perform. Surely, many believed, this god must mount the sky in a golden chariot drawn by white horses. Or, as the Egyptians said, he might sail across the sky in a boat.

The sun was the great father-god who gave life to all living things. People worshiped this sun day after day, season after season; out of their experience came the signs and symbols through which they expressed their love and their fear.

Besides making symbols, people also told stories in an attempt to explain mysterious events like the rising and setting of the sun. Such stories are called myths. Along with the sun wheels certain patterns of mythology were imprinted forever on people's minds. One such pattern was the myth of the hero who died and came to life again, as the sun seemed to die each night and come to life at dawn.

The people who lived in very early times, in the period we call the Stone Age, had no written language. We do not know much about them, compared with what we know of people in later times. What little we have learned comes mainly from a study of tools they left behind and their paintings, sculpture, and carvings.

Deep in the dark interior of caves, lit probably by a flaming torch held in one hand, early people made paintings to help them in their struggle to stay alive. Some were pictures of the animals they wanted to hunt for food. Such pictures had a magical purpose; the hunter felt sure they would help him to find these animals when he went forth with his spear.

Other times the hunter drew circles as signs of the sun. These, too, were for magic. By painting sun circles, surely the hunter could make the sun do whatever he wished. A god as powerful as the sun might even help him to aim his spear and let it strike where it would kill.

THE SUN IN ART, THE GRAPHIS PRESS, ZURICH.

Cave drawing from Las Batuecas, Spain.

The Spanish cave drawing is the earliest we know of in which the sun is not merely a circle but a disk with rays. We are not sure of the meaning of this drawing. It may have been a kind of map, showing the sunny places where game could be found. Probably, though, it was more than that. The hunter who made it may have hoped that somehow the drawing would help the sun to climb the sky each day and bring light and warmth to the earth and all the creatures on it.

In the margin is another, somewhat later, sun sign from a Spanish cave.

People found still other ways of representing the sun. One early sun sign, found in a number of places, shows the sun with three rays. The lines at the ends of the rays represented the sky.

Much later, astronomers would use a variation of this sign to show the rising sun, and another variation to show the setting sun.

American Indians of the Late Stone Age carved on rock the version of the sun wheel you can see at the right.

A spiral was another early sign of the sun. These spirals were carved on rock in Malta.

The sun was not always represented as a circle. Early people of Mesopotamia showed it as an eye. To many people the sun-god must have seemed like a great eye in the heavens, looking down upon the earth.

All through history people have made signs to express their feeling about the sun. They have cut these signs into stone and wood, hammered and engraved them in metal, drawn and painted them on rocks, paper, and canvas.

This is a book about these signs and symbols of the sun and about some of the myths that explain the symbols.

II. THE SUMERIANS AND THE EGYPTIANS WORSHIPED THE SUN

The earliest people lived by hunting wild animals and gathering grains and fruits that grew nearby. For hundreds of thousands of years this was the only way of life they knew. But in time people learned to plant the seeds of the wild grain and other plants they had used for food. They could then grow their own grain and fruits in their own gardens.

Day after day, season by season, these early farmers watched the sun. It was even more important to them than it had been to hunting people. The sun was the farmers' clock and their calendar. Seeds must be planted at the right season. They would grow in the warmth of the sun, and in due time the crops would be ready to harvest.

To early farmers the sun was a symbol of light and life. It was a great god in the sky. Ceremonies were performed to please the sun. People offered him their prayers. To many people it was the sun-god above all who gave meaning to their lives.

He was the center of their religion.

Some of the earliest people we know much about were the Sumerians. They lived in Mesopotamia, a land in Asia Minor between two rivers, the Tigris and the Euphrates.

The Sumerians believed that the sun was a god named Shamash, son of Sin, the moon-god. Each morning Shamash was said to emerge from the heavy gates in the Mountain of the East. Rays of light shone from his shoulders. His faithful driver, Bunene, then drove him up, up into the sky in a blaze of light. All day the chariot traveled across the sky. One of its wheels was a flaming disk. It was this that people on earth saw in the sky and called the sun. In the evening Shamash would disappear through the great door of the Mountain of the West. All night he would journey underground, and at dawn he would again emerge through the Mountain of the East.

The Sumerian sun-god, Shamash. A large sun disk rests on an altar before him.

BRITISH MUSEUM, LONDON.

Shamash himself was a symbol of light. But he did more than light the world each day. His piercing rays helped him to see into the future; he knew what was about to happen everywhere on earth. He could see crimes that were planned by evildoers, and his rays would make a web to entangle them.

The sun-god Ra was at the very center of the religion of the ancient Egyptians. It was Ra who ruled the earth. He was so powerful and so complicated a god that he was given many names and many shapes. Countless legends were told about Ra, and he appeared in symbolic form over and over again in paintings and writing and sculpture. Sometimes he was represented by a simple disk, sometimes by a hawk or by a disk with a hawk's wings or by other creatures—a beetle, a phoenix, a lion, or a cat. The stories and the beliefs varied from place to place, and they changed with the passing of time. But though the Egyptians believed in many gods, the god of the sun remained supreme.

The Egyptians believed that the sun-god made his great journey across the sky in a boat with gracefully curved posts at bow and stern. He was called Ra in the heat of midday. At sunset he merged with Osiris, god of all growing plants. Osiris as sun-god spent each night fighting huge

The Egyptian sun-god, Ra, in his boat.

evil serpents in the mist and darkness. In the morning the sun-god would appear as Horus, the ancient god of the sky. Horus took the form of a sacred hawk as he lit the sky at dawn.

To the Egyptians this daily journey of the sun symbolized the struggle between the powers of Light and Life and the power of Darkness. This was a struggle that the people felt going on within themselves. When the sun reappeared each morning as the glorious young Horus, people rejoiced. Evil had been conquered during the long night. Good had triumphed, and by midday the great god Ra would shine down again on the broad fields of Egypt beside the River Nile. The grain would ripen and life would go on.

Sometimes, it was said, Horus assumed the form of a great disk, ancient symbol of the sun. One morning, with his hawk's wings flapping out on each side of the disk, Horus flew up to the sun to wage war against the enemies of the god Ra.

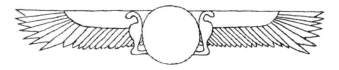

Wildly he descended upon these enemies and destroyed them all.

This story is the source of one of the most famous Egyptian symbols of the sun, a disk with outstretched wings. Carved in stone, it was often placed over the doors of temples and other buildings, where it was supposed to banish evil. On the entrances of tombs it was meant to protect the dead from harm. Because it was first of all a sun symbol, it may also have signified life after death when it was used on tombs. The Egyptians believed that the human soul was born again after death, just as the sun appeared each day at dawn, though it had seemed to die the night before.

The disk, or circle, was of course a very early symbol of the sun, known in many parts of the world. In Egyptian writing the hieroglyph, or written sign, for sun was a circle with a dot in its center. This may have represented an egg, with the dot signifying the new life within it. The Egyptians sometimes represented the sun as an egg that was laid every morning by a Great Sky Goose.

The dot within a circle is still used by astronomers and astrologers as a sign meaning the sun. It is also the Chinese sign for the sun.

The disk of the sun appears often in Egyptian painting and sculpture. Sometimes the sun-god was portrayed as a bright disk with rays ending in small hands, as if to show that the sun gave life to the world.

There were still other Egyptian symbols for the sun. Ra was sometimes a beetle rolling before him a flaming ball that was the sun. This idea came from the Egyptians' observation of the scarab beetle which rolled its egg about in a ball of earth. They believed the beetle created itself in this ball. So, too, the sun re-created itself each day.

In some parts of Egypt a cat-goddess named Bast was worshiped as daughter and wife of the sun-god. Egyptian paintings often showed a cat biting off the head of the serpent of darkness, while Ra himself, or another form of the sun-god, looked on with approval. Any Egyptian who killed a cat, whether intentionally or not, was sentenced to die.

Other creatures were associated with the sun by the ancient Egyptians. One was the fabulous phoenix. From very early times this mythological bird had symbolized life on earth and life after death. When the phoenix had lived five hundred years or more, people said, it would make for itself a secret nest of rare spices. In the heat of the sun, fanned by the wings of the bird, the nest would burst into flames. The phoenix would be reduced to ashes, but from these ashes it would arise, young again, ready to begin the same pattern of life, death, and rebirth. In Egypt the phoenix

On facing page:
The cat-goddess named Bast.

Panel showing Horus, god of the sun at dawn, and a scarab beetle, representing the sun-god Ra.

METROPOLITAN MUSEUM OF ART, NEW YORK.

was still another form of the sun-god Ra.

The famous sphinx of Egypt is yet another form of Horus. A number of statues of the sphinx still exist, but the most famous is at Gizeh. It is a huge stone lion with a human head, facing the rising sun, which it symbolizes. The sphinx was meant as a colossal home for the spirit of the sun-god, where the god could dwell while he watched over the souls of the dead.

On facing page:
The Pharaoh Tut-ankh-amun
and his wife. Note the small hands
at the ends of the sun's rays.

Below: An Egyptian sphinx.

It was believed that the Egyptian king, the Pharaoh, was himself a sun-god, directly descended from Ra. The Pharaohs built their own tombs.

These were pyramids, enormous stone structures pointing upward toward the sun. The Pharaohs built obelisks, too, four-sided tapering shafts of stone that reached for the sky and were symbols of the rays of the sun. One obelisk, called Cleopatra's Needle, was presented by Egypt to the United States in the nineteenth century. It stands in Central Park in New York City, sixty-nine feet high and weighing two hundred tons. Two other Cleopatra's Needles had been cut from the same piece of stone. One was presented to England and one to France.

One Egyptian Pharaoh, Akhenaten, is remembered above all because he proclaimed that there were not many gods, but only one, Ra the sun-god. Akhenaten built a city for Ra, a glorious city of the sun. There each morning Akhenaten the Pharaoh celebrated the rising of the sun. At night his wife Nefertiti celebrated its setting. Akhenaten did not doubt that he himself was divine, a son of Ra. But he believed that all people were brothers, whether Egyptians or foreigners, whether men or women.

Akhenaten composed a great hymn to the sun. Here is part of it (Aten was Akhenaten's name for the sun-god):

You rise glorious at the heavens' edge, O living
  Aten!
You in whom all life began.
When you shone from the eastern horizon
You filled every land with your beauty. . . .
You have made far skies so that you may shine
  in them,
Your disk in its solitude looks on all that you have
  made,
Appearing in its glory and gleaming both near
  and far.
Out of your singleness you shape a million forms—
Towns and villages, fields, roads and the river.
All eyes behold you, bright Disk of the day.

Akhenaten's bright city, his single god, and his
ideas of brotherhood were the greatest tribute to
the great Ra that had ever been made. But Akhenaten failed. The Egyptians were not ready to
believe in one god or in peace and brotherhood.
No other Pharaohs followed Akhenaten's way. Ra
remained a symbol of light and life, but in Egypt
after Akhenaten's time the sun was never again
worshiped as a single god of the universe.

Akhenaten with his queen, Nefertiti.
Again, a sun with small hands at the ends
of its rays gives life to the world.

III. PERSIAN, GREEK, AND ROMAN SUN SYMBOLS

Nowhere in the ancient world of Europe and Asia was the sun-god as important as in Egypt. But other people worshiped the sun in their own way, and for everyone it was a symbol of life and light. In some religions there was no god devoted solely to the sun. Nevertheless the followers of these religions felt that only a god could control the sun in its journey across the sky.

In ancient Persia, the greatest god of all was Ahura Mazda, creator of the earth and all its creatures. This god was also master of the heavens; the sun, the moon, and the stars were at his command. The symbol of Ahura Mazda was a disk with wings, like that of the Egyptian god Horus.

The Persian god Mithra was more directly concerned with the sun. He was a god of light, closely associated with Ahura Mazda. Mithra was said to journey across the sky each day in a chariot pulled by four white horses. Like the chariot of the

Sumerian sun-god Shamash, Mithra's chariot had one flaming wheel, symbol of the sun's bright light. Mithra's flaming wheel shone with precious gems. He was god of "the unconquered sun."

A poet of ancient Persia wrote in his "Hymn to the Sun":

We sacrifice unto the undying, shining, swift-horsed Sun. . . .
I will sacrifice unto Mithra, the lord of wide pastures, who has a thousand ears, ten thousand eyes. . . .
I will sacrifice unto that friendship, the best of all friendships, that reigns between the moon and the sun.
I bless the sacrifice and the invocation, and the strength and vigour of the undying, shining, swift-horsed Sun.

Other Persian gods were sometimes associated with the sun. Marduk, who had a human form, made the plants grow and the grain ripen. He symbolized the sun of springtime, when all the world seems to come alive again. Nergal symbolized the hot sun of midsummer. He was represented by a lion.

The gods of the ancient Greeks were very much like people. They were capable of great deeds, but often they quarreled, they stole, they lied to one another. The Greeks were seldom afraid of these all-too-human gods.

One of the most ancient and respected of the Greek gods was Helios, god of the sun. Every morning Helios was said to emerge from a swamp formed by the river at the edge of the ocean, in the distant East where the Ethiopians lived. He would climb up the sky in his golden chariot drawn by nine winged fire-breathing white horses. Both gods and men welcomed the light of the day as Helios swept along. His golden helmet shone; his eyes flashed. Dazzling beams of light shot out from his chest. His body was draped in shining garments, whipped by the wind.

At the end of his journey Helios seemed to plunge into the ocean. But that is not what really happened, the Greeks said. At the edge of the western ocean Helios found his mother, his wife, and his children waiting for him in a golden boat with sails. Or, as some tales said, they waited in a huge cup made of gold. All night Helios would sail with them through the darkness until he reached the swamp at the edge of the ocean. From this swamp he would again climb the sky with his white horses to bring the light of day to all the world.

Helios, like the Sumerian sun-god Shamash, could see everything that happened on earth and in the sky. Nothing escaped him; the misdeeds of the gods were no exception. In one famous Greek myth it was Helios who informed Demeter, goddess of the cultivated earth, that her daughter Persephone had been stolen by Pluto, dark god of the underworld.

Helios was a symbol of the sun, but he was more than that; he *was* the sun. The Greeks portrayed him, driving his chariot across the sky, on some of their most beautiful vases. In one such painting the stars are shown as boys diving into the sea. The sun-god in his chariot was also portrayed in sculpture on the temple called the Parthenon. There he represented the eastern sky at dawn.

At the entrance to the harbor of the city of Rhodes the Greeks placed a bronze statue of Helios, so huge that ships in full sail could pass between its legs. Called the Colossus of Rhodes, it was one of the seven wonders of the ancient world. It stood for a little more than fifty years before it was destroyed by an earthquake.

Many tales were told about Helios. Perhaps the most famous is the story of Phaëthon, son of Helios, who obtained from his father the promise to let him drive Helios's chariot across the sky. This was too much of a task for Phaëthon; he could not manage the white horses of the sun.

The Colossus of Rhodes as imagined, much later,
by a seventeenth century engraver.
Latin at top reads: Colossus, sun at Rhodes.

Unrestrained, the horses raced off into unknown regions of the sky among the stars, then down so close to earth that woods and fields, villages and cities were scorched. The goddess of the earth herself was overcome with heat and thirst. The frightened people hid themselves in the deepest caves. At last Zeus, chief of all the gods, hurled his mighty thunderbolt, to keep the world from going up in flames. Phaëthon fell headlong to his death, like a shooting star.

Another Greek god, Phoebus Apollo, was originally a god of light, without being the sun itself. He was a son of Zeus. When Apollo was born on the little Greek island of Delos, a cock crowed, herald of the sunrise. The rocky foundations of the island were said to have turned to gold. So did all the olive trees. All day a golden light shone from a round pool on the island.

As god of light Apollo helped make the fruits of the earth ripen. He was represented as a strong and handsome man with long hair hanging loose and a wreath of bay leaves on his head. He carried a bow and arrow and a lyre for making music. In Greek literature there are descriptions of Apollo playing his lyre while other gods and goddesses danced. He was "beautiful and tall . . . alight with radiance. Brightly shone his feet and his raiment."

Just as the sun can bring life, but also death

with its scorching rays, so Apollo was more than a god of light. He was thought of as an archer who shot arrows from afar, causing sudden death. (In Greek literature arrows are often symbols of sunbeams.) He could also heal the ills of people on earth and drive away evil. Like sun-gods of other countries, he could foretell the future.

As people traveled from one country to another in the ancient world, they took their ideas and their customs with them. So it was that the Greek god Apollo became the bright symbol of the sun for the people of Rome, and a wheel of his chariot was thought to be the sun itself.

The first Roman emperor, Augustus, chose the radiant Apollo as his guardian and protector and built a temple in his honor.

A later Roman emperor, Heliogabalus, had his own strange symbol of the sun, a large black cone-shaped stone. This stone was said to have fallen from the sky and to be an image of the sun itself. Heliogabalus (the first part of whose name was meant to suggest the Greek sun-god Helios) had the stone brought from a temple in Syria, Asia Minor. In Rome he built for this sun symbol an impressive temple surrounded by many altars. Animals were sacrificed daily to the god on these altars, incense was burned, wine was poured about. The emperor, along with a choir of Syrian girls, then danced before the altar to the rhythm of clashing cymbals and beating drums.

In the heat of summer, this symbol of the sun was escorted out of Rome in a chariot glistening with gold and jewels, drawn by six white horses. The road was strewn with gold dust, and the crowds along the way waved torches and scattered flowers. The god, still in the shape of this black stone, was then taken to his second temple, located in a pleasant suburb where he would not suffer from excessive heat—of course, his own heat. These gaudy ceremonies were a way of worshiping the sun, or its symbol, but it was a pompous and superficial kind of worship.

Meanwhile, the cult of Mithraism had found its way to Rome. Elaborate ceremonies accompanied the worship of the Persian god Mithra. Fragrance of incense rose into the air, and choirs chanted sacred music. Bulls were sacrificed to the god. One day of the Roman week was dedicated to Mithra, and one day of the year, December 25, was celebrated as the birthday of "the unconquered sun." This was approximately the time of the winter solstice, when the days of winter begin to grow longer. December 25, of course, was to become an important date for Christians.

The unconquered sun who never grows old was popular with many ancient people, and especially with soldiers, who saw him as the eternal warrior who could not only win battles but conquer the evil on the earth. And as Mithra did not die, so, too, death on earth might not be the end of life for those who believed in him.

Half a century after the time of Heliogabalus, the Roman Emperor Aurelian decreed that the cult of *Sol Invictus* (Latin for "unconquered sun") should be the state religion of the Roman Empire. He himself wore a golden diadem; he was a symbol of the sun. A later emperor, Diocletian, dressed in golden robes and demanded that people prostrate themselves before him as representative of the sun. He consecrated a temple to Mithra, great protector of the empire.

Mithraism was a religion rich in symbolism. Roman carvings of this period show twin boys standing beside the god, each holding a torch. One torch points up to represent the rising sun. The other points down, as the sun sets. The sun itself was of course the greatest symbol of all, for followers of Mithra as for many other people.

The armies of Rome had conquered most of the known Western world. People from far and near, of many different races and beliefs, had settled in this great city. Whatever their beliefs, most could accept this worship of the undying sun. It seemed to them that this light in the sky would guide their lives and bring them warmth, not only from without but in their hearts and minds.

IV. THE SCANDINAVIANS CARVED ON ROCK

In many parts of the world people believed that the sun-god made his daily journey in a golden chariot. Usually the chariot was pulled by white horses and they, too, became symbols of the sun. We have already seen that this was true of the Sumerians, the Persians, the Greeks, and the Romans.

Much the same belief was held by the Scandinavians who lived in northern Europe. The people of this region have always had a special feeling for the sun. In much of the area where they live winter lasts for more than half the year and the nights are very long. The sun is welcomed with joy and thanksgiving each day as it breaks through the winter dark.

We know a great deal about the Egyptians, Greeks, and other people who lived near the Mediterranean Sea in ancient times because they left many written records and a copious literature. This is not true of the Scandinavians who lived north of them at about the same time. But the Scandinavians did leave behind them many fascinating carvings on the rocks of their homeland. They did not do their carving in caves. Instead, they chose, when they could, smooth and gently sloping rocks facing wide fields.

These carvings, and also objects that have been found, tell us something about the feeling these northern people had for the sun. For them, too, the sun was a symbol of light and life. Sun worship was apparently an important part of their religion.

The sun, they believed, must make its daily journey across the sky in a chariot drawn by horses. But important as this was in their lives, the Scandinavians seem to have been even more concerned about the sun's journey during the long, cold nights. The sun was weakened, they thought, by the cold and the darkness. Unseen, it traveled all night in a ship through the dangerous waters of the underworld. People felt they must do what they could to help the sun survive the perils of the long winter nights. They must help it to gain enough strength so that winter at last would end and the earth would again grow green.

Probably ceremonies were held to aid the sun-god. People may have acted out the arrival of the sun at dawn, using a ship that carried a disk to represent the sun. Rock carvings show ships, most of them bearing a sun disk. These are evidently records of religious dramas. There are many; two are shown in the margin.

In one carving of a ship, the sun disk is supported on two legs. Three men are shown dancing around it, brandishing axes, for what purpose we do not know, though the sun itself was sometimes represented by an ax. Human figures above the ship are upside down. They may have been acrobats taking part in the sun ceremony. Possibly, though, the man who made this carving placed them high above the ship because the scene was becoming too crowded.

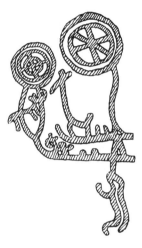

Here is a carving in which the sun disk, supported on a single leg, is carried in a ship that seems to be drawn by a horse, or at least to have a horse as its figurehead.

Chariots are common in rock carvings, too. Here is a stylized carving of a sun chariot. The wheels of the chariot itself look like sun disks, but probably the disk attached to the end of the pole was meant to represent the sun.

In another carving the sun disk appears to be unattached.

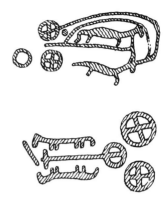

Rock carvings survived better than other forms of art in Scandinavia. They were seldom smashed and most of them could not be carried away. However, a beautiful relic of early times was discovered in a bog in Denmark. It is a small chariot of the sun, made of bronze and gold, dating back to one thousand years or more before the time of Christ. Six wheels, only one of them intact, hold up a framework that carries a sun disk engraved on both sides with circles and spirals. Gold plating still remains on one side of the bronze disk.

In front of the disk stands a charming horse, with rays radiating from his eyes, as if they, too, were symbols of the sun. This is not a prancing horse; he seems quite still. The whole setup of chariot and horse is about two feet long. It may have been pulled along in a ceremonial procession. Wheels, disks, circles, and spirals, everything about the chariot suggests worship of the sun.

Disks of the sun took many forms in Scandinavia. They are frequently found in rock carvings, often by themselves, without boat or chariot. To

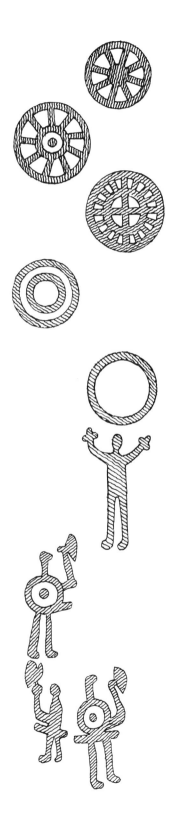

the left are some typical designs, from Sweden.

How do we know that these are sun disks rather than just pictures of wheels? How do we know they are religious symbols, since these people left no writings about their carvings? To answer these questions, anthropologists consider what else they know about the Scandinavians of this period. They think about the sun symbols of other people—the Greeks, the Romans, even the people of India. For it is known that in quite early times there were massive movements of people from one part of Asia or Europe to another. It is probably no accident that similar sun wheels have been found in places far apart from one another, and that many ancient people of Europe and Asia believed that the sun crossed the sky each day in a horse-drawn chariot.

There is another reason for believing that the Scandinavian sun disks are religious symbols. They are often accompanied by a human figure with arms raised in prayer.

Scandinavians must have found in the sun disks a symbol that expressed, better than words, their feeling of joy and wonder at the warmth and light bestowed on them by the god of the sun.

There are also carvings of disk men, figures in which sun disks are combined with more or less human features. These may represent worshipers bearing the symbol of the sun.

Brooch with curving swastika design.

NATIONAL MUSEUM, COPENHAGEN.

Walking disks can be quite fanciful, as you can see in the drawing at the left.

Sometimes, it seems, the sun-god came down to earth and left his symbolic footprints on the rocks.

The sun disk remained an important symbol in Scandinavia for many years. It appeared on decorated metalwork, including sword scabbards and jewelry. In time, the disk was replaced by the swastika as a symbol of the turning sun. In Denmark a lovely brooch made of bronze and iron was discovered in a centuries-old grave. It was decorated with sun disks and a curving swastika.

At the bottom of the page is a swastika on a memorial stone. The ends of this swastika have been joined to form a continuous pattern.

The chariot of the sun was remembered, too. In the Edda poems, collected in Iceland about the year 1200 after Christ, we read of two horses drawing the sun's chariot. One is called Arvakr, the Early-Waker. The other is Alsvior, the All-Strong.

The mythology of these northern people, written down long after the carvings were made on the rocks, tells of gods associated with the sun. Odin, the all-father, controlled the high heavens; the sun was sometimes referred to as his eye. Balder, a son of Odin, was the much-loved god of springtime, sunlight, and gladness. He was said

to die at midsummer, the time of the summer solstice. Bright fires of pine branches were kindled to light his way to the underworld. Six months later, at the winter solstice, Balder was born again as the sun began to move higher in the sky each day. People burned huge logs and hung lights on fir trees to help Balder, the sun hero, on his way.

Another son of Odin, Thor, the thunderer, ruled the clouds. He crossed the sky in a wagon drawn by goats. Its wheels rolled along with a noise of thunder; bright sparks shot from those wheels.

Remnants of early sun worship exist in many parts of western Europe. Circular tombs dating back to prehistoric times have been found and excavated; there are many in Ireland. A typical one is Newgrange, about thirty miles north of Dublin near the river Boyne. This is a "passage-grave"; so-called because the burial chamber is entered through a long passageway. It dates back to about two thousand years before Christ, a time when stone, not metal, was the everyday material for tools and weapons in Ireland.

A circle of stone slabs makes a curb around the burial mound at Newgrange. Tremendous standing stones, six to eight feet high, once formed a huge circle outside the tomb. There must have been from thirty-five to thirty-eight of these stones; only twelve are still there.

We have no way of knowing for certain whether these circles were connected with sun worship, but it does seem likely. Sun worship was widespread among early people. Besides, there is other evidence. A number of the stones are decorated with graceful spiral designs that must have been made by picking out grooves with a sharp stone. A spiral is a very early symbol of the sun.

Each year thousands of people from all over the world visit Stonehenge on Salisbury Plain in southern England. This is a Stone Age monument made of huge rough-cut stones. Many of the stones have fallen from their original upright position; others were carried away to be used in building bridges and mill dams. But enough were left so that experts could figure out the original plan fairly accurately. There was an outer circle of big stones and an inner one of smaller "blue stones." Inside these circles were two horseshoe-shaped sets of stones. At the center curve of the horseshoes stood an altar stone, and near it a stone marker that shed its shadow exactly on the altar on Midsummer Day, a day near the beginning of the summer solstice, which occurs on June 21 by our calendar.

The entrance of the horseshoes faced a ceremonial avenue that extended toward the point on the horizon where the sun rose on the day of the

solstice. Photographs taken on this day in recent years show a bright circle of reflected sunlight against the stones of the outer circle, as the sun rises above the altar.

Stonehenge had many passageways, many openings through which a watcher could study the sky. It may have been used for measuring the rising and setting of the moon and the stars. Astronomers have found that eclipses of the sun and moon could have been predicted there. But though we have no positive proof of this, Stonehenge must

BRITISH TOURIST AUTHORITY.

surely have been above all a temple to the sun-god himself. How else can we explain the rising of the sun over the altar stone at the summer solstice? The sun worship of these early people was very likely a part of the cult of the sun that reached from Egypt and India across Europe and, as we shall see, included also people far across the ocean to the west.

In time, the people of northern and western Europe adopted the Christian religion. They no longer worshiped the sun. Many of the ancient symbols lived on in their customs and celebrations just the same. In some places a cartwheel covered with straw was set on fire and rolled downhill in a springtime festival. If it kept on burning all the way down, the grain would grow well and there would be an abundant harvest. This blazing wheel was surely a sun wheel.

In other places boys threw flaming disks of wood into the air. Great bonfires were built on the hills on the first day of May or soon thereafter. These, too, represented the sun. Warmed by the many fires, the sun would become stronger and make the grain grow tall in the fields. People danced around the fires, leaping as high as they could. This they believed would also make the grain grow high. In their dancing, people moved in the same direction the sun followed as it crossed the sky.

This springtime fire festival was called *Beltane,* a word that meant bright fire. In later times there would be more fires and dancing and burning wheels on Midsummer Eve, the night before the summer solstice. Customs such as these lasted into the present century, long after most of the people who followed them had become Christians. The power of the sun, great symbol of light and growth, was not forgotten.

V. HEBREW AND
CHRISTIAN SUN SYMBOLISM

The Hebrews of Palestine in ancient times were absolutely forbidden to worship the sun. Their religious leaders made this clear to them. They were also told they must not worship idols of any kind. Indeed, the second of the Ten Commandments states: "Thou shalt not make unto thee any graven image, or any likeness of any thing that is in heaven above, or that is in the earth beneath, or that is in the water under the earth. Thou shalt not bow down thyself to them, nor serve them. . . ."

To be sure, there were Hebrews who bowed down to the idols of their neighbors; there were also those who practiced magic. The great prophets stormed against such doings. There is only one God, they said; He is a God of righteousness, Lord of the universe. People listened to the prophets, and the Hebrew religion became a religion of righteousness.

Still, it was impossible for the Hebrews to avoid

being influenced by the beliefs of neighboring peoples. Palestine was on the highroad between Egypt and the major countries of Asia. There was a constant exchange of ideas. The Hebrews knew about the great god of light worshiped by the Persians and other nations to the east. The idea of a god of light was not unfamiliar to them. The prophet Isaiah had said, "The Lord shall be thine everlasting light."

Many Greeks settled in Palestine after it was conquered by the armies of Alexander the Great in 332 B.C. Many Hebrews were influenced by the Greeks. Later, in 63 B.C., came the Roman armies. Greek and Roman ideas were in the air.

There were Hebrews who kept their religion untouched by outside influences. There were others who adapted some of the pagan beliefs to their own way of worship. In a Hebrew book of magic called *The Book of Mysteries*, dated third century A.D., we find a prayer to the Greek sun-god Helios. It is written in Greek words spelled with Hebrew letters.

The Hebrews of ancient times did not produce much great architecture, sculpture, or painting. They were hindered by the second commandment. But in later centuries there was a change. To some of the Jews (as they were then called) it no longer seemed wrong to make a likeness of things on the earth or in heaven. In the State

of Israel (Palestine until recent times) a number
of mosaic floors of old synagogues have been uncovered. (A mosaic is a design or picture made
of small squares of colored glass or stone, set in
cement.) Some of these mosaics actually represent pagan gods.

The illustration shows the center of a mosaic
on the floor of a synagogue dating to about A.D.
520. It was excavated in the 1920s at Beth Alpha
in Palestine. The Greek sun-god Helios is shown

driving his chariot; certainly he is a likeness of a thing "in heaven above." Two wheels of the chariot are at the bottom of the circle, facing front. The four horses are represented by just their faces and forelegs. Helios himself has an elaborate halo in gold and red and white. He is truly a god of light, seemingly more Greek than Hebrew.

The early Christians believed in one God, ruler of heaven and earth, as did the Hebrews of Palestine. This God could not be seen, as could the sun, but he could be felt in the hearts of people who knew and loved him. The Christians believed that Jesus Christ was the Son of God who had come to live on earth so that people could find new life.

Though Jesus himself was a Hebrew, most of the Hebrews did not become Christians. It was in Rome that the church grew and finally prospered. At first there were very few Christians, and they were often persecuted by the pagans among whom they lived. But as time went on, more and more people joined this new cult that preached love and the brotherhood of all humankind.

Life became easier for the Christians under the Roman Emperor Constantine in the fourth century A.D. Constantine declared himself a Christian; all people, he said, had a right to follow the religion of their choice.

The Roman Emperor Theodosius carried his Christianity a bit further. He decreed that everyone must be a Christian. The whole Roman calendar of festivals and other religious events was to be abolished. Christian festivals were to take their place. There would be no more worship of the sun, whether he was named Helios or Apollo or Sol Invictus.

Still, many of the Christians had followed the cult of Mithra; others had worshiped Apollo. The sun had been their god. And there in the bright sky, day after day, shone the same sun that had brought life to the world since time began. It is not surprising that the early Christians often confused the ancient god of the sun with Christ. After all, the birth of Christ was like the rising of the sun, bringing light to the world. It was hard to believe that this sun in the sky was merely a symbol of Christ, not Christ himself.

The special Christian day of the week, too, had long been called the "day of the Sun," though the church favored the Latin name, *Dominica,* "Lord's Day."

Later, when Christians began to read the Bible, they discovered these words of the prophet Malachi: "The sun of righteousness shall rise, with healing in its wings." This, they thought, was surely a prediction of the coming of Christ. The sun and Christ were after all much the same. (You

may remember that the winged disk was an ancient symbol of the sun-god.)

In the New Testament, Christ was described thus: "His face did shine as the sun, and his raiment was white as the light."

A striking example of the identification of the sun-god with Christ was discovered in the 1950s when archaeologists, digging in Rome in search of historical relics, uncovered an early Christian mosaic. This mosaic shows Christ as the sun driving a chariot, with a cloak flying from his shoulders. About his head are rays of bright light in a circle.

Numerous pictures made at this time and later showed Christ rising into the sky after his resurrection from the dead. Often he rode in a fiery chariot, like a sun-god driving across the sky.

The picture of a German tombstone of about the sixth or seventh century A.D. also shows Christ as a sun-god. Sun rays make a halo all around his head and there are still more rays behind him. These are sun symbols, pagan and Christian at the same time.

Try as they would, the priests could not persuade the people to give up all the rituals and other customs that had been part of pagan worship for thousands of years. Little by little the church adapted these customs to Christian beliefs.

Pagan festivals became part of the Christian year.

For thousands of years the winter solstice had been considered a time for rejoicing. The lengthening of the days gave proof that, after all, the sun had not deserted humankind; warmer days would come. In Rome, a gay festival called the Saturnalia was held at this time, in honor of Saturn, god of the sowing of the grain. The Saturnalia lasted seven days, ending on December 23. To followers of the cult of Mithra, the 25th of December was even more important; it was, as we have seen, the birthday of "the unconquered sun."

Christians at first did not celebrate the birth of Christ at any set time. No one knew exactly when he was born. But soon after the time of the Emperor Constantine, December 25 was chosen as the date. Constantine had been a worshiper of Sol Invictus before he became a Christian. As with many newly converted Christians, his religion was a mixture of pagan and Christian beliefs. It is not surprising that the feast of Sol Invictus became the birthday of Christ.

Some Christians refused to celebrate Christ's birth on a day that had for so long been dedicated to the sun, but most accepted December 25 as the date. Pagan rites and Christian festivities were held side by side. Often there was little difference between them. Houses were decorated with greenery; candles were carried in procession.

"Sol novus oritur," Christians sang in Latin at their Christmas service: "The new sun rises." Christians insisted that they celebrated not the sun in the sky that would wane each year as the days grew shorter, but the "Sun of Righteousness who . . . will never wane." But for many years the confusion between the two suns remained.

Missionaries carried Christian beliefs to other European countries. For thousands of years, to the north of Rome, fires had been lit at the time of the winter solstice and logs kindled to help warm the sun-god so the days could grow longer and crops could grow in the earth. These customs, too, became a part of Christmas. The blazing log was later transformed into our yule log.

Other celebrations in the Christian year follow the cycle of the sun. The date of Easter depends on both the sun and the moon. For this celebration the church chose the "day of the Sun" following the first full moon after the spring equinox, which is about March 21. At this time day and night are of equal length.

In the spring the earth seemed to come alive again. New leaves uncurled on the branches of trees, green shoots sprang up everywhere in the earth that had seemed so dead throughout the winter. There was a promise of blossoms, and all the fruits. Surely this was an appropriate time to celebrate the death and resurrection of Christ.

For many Christians Easter was a celebration of the sun. Christ died and rose from the dead. Just so each evening the sun seemed to die; at dawn it came to life again. Christ's resurrection was a coming to life in the springtime for people who believed in him.

It was said that the sun danced for joy at dawn on Easter. Many people rose early so they could see this happen. As they gazed at the rising sun, wide-eyed, it really did seem to dance.

In parts of Germany and England, villagers climbed a hill on Easter eve and spent the night on its top so they could perform "three bounds of joy" at sunrise, while the sun danced.

Thousands of people in our country and in Europe still gather to watch the sun rise on Easter. It is a symbol of the new light that Christ brought to the world.

Fire means light, too. The Christian Church in Europe tried to stop people from burning fires in the springtime to honor the sun-god. But fires were still lit on May Day and flaming wheels were rolled downhill. In time the church adapted this custom, too, to the Christian calendar. On Easter Eve all the lights would be put out in the church. Then a new fire would be kindled outside and the priest would bless the flames. The great Easter candle of the church was lit from this fire, and all the lights in the church were rekindled.

Gradually the worship of Sol Invictus was left behind. Now and then, to be sure, Christ was still confused with the god of the sun. A pen drawing from a French manuscript of the early fourteenth century shows Christ carrying a sun globe in his hand, riding in a four-horse chariot decorated with a cross. There were other examples, but they became fewer and fewer.

In spite of this, many solar images remained, accepted by most Christians as symbols of the light

THE SUN IN ART,
THE GRAPHIS PRESS, ZURICH.

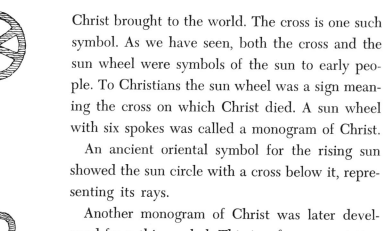

Christ brought to the world. The cross is one such symbol. As we have seen, both the cross and the sun wheel were symbols of the sun to early people. To Christians the sun wheel was a sign meaning the cross on which Christ died. A sun wheel with six spokes was called a monogram of Christ.

An ancient oriental symbol for the rising sun showed the sun circle with a cross below it, representing its rays.

Another monogram of Christ was later developed from this symbol. This is a famous variation of the cross. It is often called the *Chi Rho* because it is a combination of the first two letters in the Greek word for Christ.

The actual cross on which Christ died was a cross of suffering. The church transformed it into a symbolic cross of glory, with bright rays radiating from its center. One of these shines on the high altar of Saint Peter's Cathedral in Rome. It is a huge golden sunburst.

The Gnostics, people belonging to an early Christian sect, designed their own sun symbol, which you see at the left. This is an elaboration of the earlier sun symbol with three rays, mentioned in chapter I. Here, too, the lines at the ends of the rays represent the sky.

The halo is another sun symbol, a sun disk painted in gold, with loving care, by Christian painters, usually behind the head of Christ, his

*Madonna with halo, by the
Italian painter Fra Filippo Lippi,
fifteenth century. Note the
sun symbol behind her head.*

METROPOLITAN MUSEUM
OF ART, NEW YORK.

Rose window, Basilica of Santa Chiara, Assisi, Italy.

Keystone of an arch in a church in Berne, Switzerland.

THE SUN IN ART,
THE GRAPHIS PRESS, ZURICH.

disciples, Mary his mother, and the saints. Often, rays were painted within the disk of the halo, or a cross with equal arms might be enclosed in it. The halo symbolizes holiness.

Sun symbols are found on many church buildings. The rose window in Gothic cathedrals and other churches may not always have been intended as a symbol of the sun. And yet, as bright sunlight streams through the many-colored glass of such a window, we cannot help feeling that here, too, is a brilliant sun wheel.

The keystone of an arch in the main porch of a church in Berne, Switzerland, has a glorious sun face, carved in stone. This church was built in about the year 1500. Sun faces were often placed on the keystone of arches.

Both the sun and the moon are found carved on Christian churches in many parts of the world. Sun symbols appear in murals on the walls of some churches in New England. The one at the left combines the ancient disk of the sun with a monogram of Christ.

There is sun symbolism in the present-day ritual of the Roman Catholic Church. The round white wafer called the Host has an important place in Holy Communion. Priest and congregation partake of the Host, in separate wafers.

This round white wafer is supposed to represent the body of Christ. But it has also another meaning. It is an ancient symbol, a sun disk, sun-bread, made of light. Usually it is imprinted with a cross or a monogram of Christ. Bread used in rituals of the Mithraic cult in Rome also was imprinted with a cross. People who take part in the Holy Communion of the Christian church may feel the light of Christ's presence within them as they eat this sun-bread. Perhaps they know nothing of the long history of this symbol. But the sun that lights the world nevertheless has its place in the Holy Communion of the church.

In certain special services the Host is displayed for adoration on the altar in a monstrance. This is often a golden image of the sun raised on a pedestal. The monstrance is embellished with rays; it may be set with precious stones.

We do not now worship the sun. Yet our lives depend on this bright disk just as the lives of people always have. And somewhere within us the symbol of the sun remains, a bright light representing the best in ourselves.

It is not surprising that the sun has so often been a symbol in religion. In different ways they both bring light to the world.

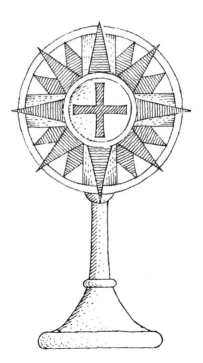

VI. SUN SYMBOLS IN OTHER PARTS OF THE WORLD

The same sun shines on all the world, but we have so far been talking almost entirely about Europe, Egypt, and western Asia. What about the rest of the world? In China, the ancient symbol of the sun was a raven in a circle. The Chinese believed that long ago the earth was lit by ten sun-ravens, one for each hour of the day. One day all ten sun-ravens appeared in the sky at once. The heat was unbearable. Plants that grew in the earth started to shrivel. People hid from the scorching heat as best they could. Then the matchless god I, the Excellent Archer, seized his bow and, aiming carefully, one by one shot down nine sun-ravens. The one that remained was from that time on the sun that lit the world.

There are other Chinese stories of the sun. In one, the sun is delivered to the sky each day in the jaws of the Dragon of the East. In another story the earth was said to be a huge chariot and the sky a curved canopy stretched above it. The sun spent the night on earth. In the morning he climbed up the branches of a sacred tree that reached to the sky.

Still, the sun-god, though he was known as the source of all light, was not greatly honored in China. People offered a sacrifice to him at the beginning of the year, and another on his birthday, but that was all. Few temples were built for the Chinese sun-god.

In Japan the sun is a goddess named Amaterasu, which means "heaven shining great deity." She is of dazzling beauty. Amaterasu was born from the left eye of the great god Izanagi, who was creator of the islands of Japan and of the gods of Wind, Trees, Mountains, Fire, and many others. Amaterasu's sister, the moon, was born from the right eye of Izanagi.

Many stories are told of Amaterasu. One of the oldest concerns the goddess and her brother Susanoo, the storm-god. Susanoo once lost all control of himself and became quite wild. He destroyed his sister's rice fields, filled in the irrigation ditches so no water could reach them, and soiled the temples. Worst of all, he broke a hole in the ceiling of the hall where Amaterasu was weaving with her ladies, and he threw down a piebald horse that he had skinned. This bloody sight so frightened one of the ladies that she pricked herself with her shuttle and fell dead.

Terrified, Amaterasu hid herself in a heavenly cave and blocked the entrance with a boulder. This was a terrible thing to do. All the world grew dark. Evil spirits ran wild everywhere. The universe itself was about to come to an end, just when it was all so new and full of possibilities.

Eight million gods and goddesses assembled in the bed of the river of heaven and drew up plans. They brought cocks to crow continuously. They decorated a tree with jewels and tied a mirror to its branches. A young goddess named Uzume did a noisy dance and the eight million gods and goddesses all laughed aloud.

Deep in her cave the sun-goddess heard the uproar. She pushed aside the boulder at the entrance a little and said, "I thought my going away made the world dark. How then can all the gods and goddesses laugh?"

Uzume replied haughtily, "We laugh because now we have a better goddess than you."

Two gods pushed forward the mirror. Amaterasu, who had never seen a mirror before, was astonished. She came part way out of the cave to look. A powerful god drew her all the way out, and a strong rope made of straw was stretched across the opening of the cave. Amaterasu could not go back.

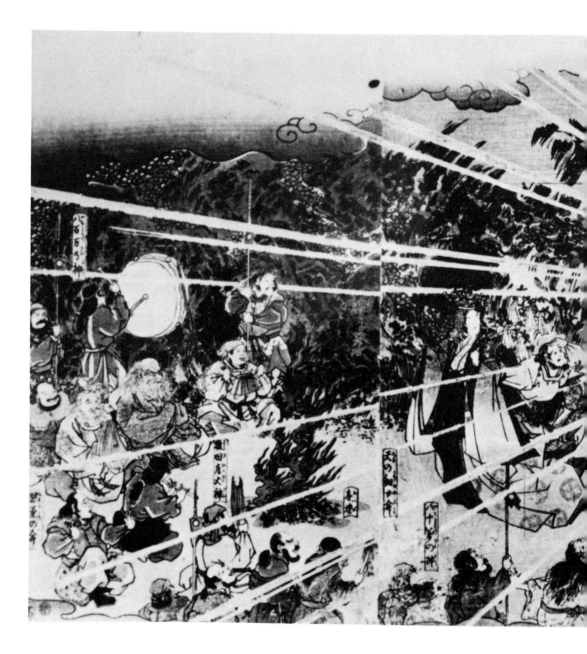

The Japanese sun-goddess Amaterasu
is lured out of her cave
by dancing gods and goddesses.

Once more all the world was lit by the rays of the beautiful sun-goddess. The sun could retreat for a time each night, as does every living thing, but it would never again disappear entirely.

The round mirror, reflecting the light of the sun-goddess herself, became her symbol. The rope of straw that was stretched across the opening of the cave when the goddess reappeared is also a symbol. It represents a feeling of joy and warmth because light has returned to the earth. Replicas of this special rope are hung above the entrances of temples and strung across the streets at the Japanese New Year festival. New Year means a new life for everyone. The sacred rope, Shimenawa, means a new world rescued from the darkness.

A sun-goddess is, after all, different from a sun-god. In the tales that are told of Amaterasu there is a way of looking at the world that is quite different from anything we find in tales of a solar-god. There is a feeling of quiet gratitude for all lovely things that are lit by the sun, a gentleness toward the gift of light.

Amaterasu is at the center of a religious cult in Japan called Shinto. The sun is adored by religious Japanese people as a living god, much as Akhenaten adored his Aten in ancient Egypt. When the bright sun rises at dawn, lighting and warming all the world, it is like a living being. At the same time it is a symbol of the divine spirit that lives in all things, from the pots and pans in the kitchen to the Emperor himself. All of the imperial family in Japan was said to be descended from the sun-goddess; the Emperor was adored as a sun-king.

The Emperor no longer rules in Japan; no one now believes that he is descended from the sun-goddess. And yet, the rising sun is still thought of as the national symbol of Japan. And there on the Japanese national flag is a big red circle, a sun disk, symbol of the bright goddess who brings the dawn.

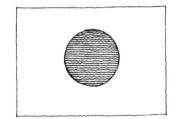

Much of the land of India is flooded with sunshine. Every part of the lives of the people depends on this hot sun, yet it has also the power to destroy the earth when it shines down day after day and no rain falls.

The people of India first worshiped this power in the sky in very early times. An ancient book on Indian painting says that the sun-god should be worshiped through its symbol, an eight-petaled lotus flower drawn on the ground. Other early Indian books speak of drawing a circle on the ground as a symbol of the sun; the god could be worshiped inside the circle. Many followers of the Hindu religion in India still begin their day with a prayer to this sun-god.

As in Egypt, the sun in India was worshiped

under many names and in many forms. Tales of the sun-god varied from place to place and changed with time. Stories of the gods are contained in the Vedas, the earliest holy books of the Hindu religion. Each of the four Vedas is a large collection of prayers, chants or hymns, and comments. It was believed that the wisdom of the Vedas came directly from the gods, the "shining ones."

In the Vedas, Surya was the god of the sun itself. He was the son of Dyaus, lord of the wide-spreading sky. His hair was golden; his arms, too, were of gold. Every day Surya rode across the sky in a golden chariot drawn by seven white mares. He could drive away the powers of darkness, witches, disease, and bad dreams.

Ushas, daughter of Heaven and sister of Night, symbolized the dawn. The poets sang of her beauty in the Vedas. Ushas, they said, wore crimson robes, with veils of gold. She was like a gentle bride or a wife who seemed more beautiful to her husband each morning. Her shining chariot was drawn by seven ruddy cows.

Savitar represented the sun in the morning and at evening. He was seen riding in his golden chariot between heaven and earth. Each day he commanded Night to approach, so that men could rest from their work, birds could sleep in their nests, and cattle could find shelter in their sheds.

*The sun-god Surya
in his chariot, from an
Indian manuscript.*

Each morning he woke the world from sleep and all the people in it. Without him the sun could not move; Surya could not cross the sky in his chariot. Nevertheless, in later times Savitar became less important; he was considered just one part of Surya.

Mitra was also associated with the sun. He was god of the growing grain and at one time also guardian of the day. We have heard of this god before; he became the Persian sun-god Mithra.

Meanwhile the ages-old symbols of the sun continued to have meaning. In India, the eight-petaled lotus flower that was drawn on the ground

for worship in very early times was a kind of sun wheel. At the time of the Vedas, too, the sun wheel represented the power of the sun. In later times the swastika became the symbol of the sun-god Surya; this, too, was a form of the sun wheel.

A temple dedicated to Surya, at Konarak in the province of Orissa, was built in the shape of a giant sun-chariot with twelve great pairs of stone wheels, each ten feet across. Each wheel is covered with minute circular carvings of flowers, rosettes, and leaves.

The followers of the Buddhist religion in India made the sun wheel their own wheel of the law, formed, as they said, "of a thousand spokes darting out a thousand rays." In time this wheel was patterned with just eight spokes, representing the eightfold path of right behavior that Buddhists said people should follow. This wheel of the law was no longer thought of as a sun wheel, but that was its origin, just the same.

A *mandala* is a design that may have as its central shape a star, a golden flower, or the circle of the sun. The word means "magic circle," but the mandala may also be a square. A mandala is used by Hindus and other Eastern people as an aid in meditation. Concentrating on the shapes in a mandala makes it easier to shut out the outside world and turn thoughts and feelings inward to-

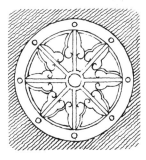

*Part of the golden ceiling in
the Golden Temple of Amritsar, India.*

ward the center of one's being. The circle, especially, enclosed as it is, keeps thoughts from scattering outward.

The magic circle is a very ancient form of the sun wheel. When early people raised their arms in worship to the sun they may have felt the way people do when they contemplate a mandala.

One form of mandala is called by the Hindus a *yantra;* it is a pattern of various shapes, at least one of them a circle. To the right is a drawing of a yantra.

It seems certain that mandala symbols came originally from dreams and visions. Such a symbol would appear to a person in a dream, then the dreamer would draw it or paint it for other people to see and contemplate. Mandalas are among the oldest religious symbols of humankind and have been found everywhere in the world.

Sand paintings made by the Indians of our Southwest are mandalas. The so-called hex signs that decorate barns in Pennsylvania Dutch country may have originally been mandalas, descended from the earliest symbols of the sun. Today, however, they are most often thought of as just signs for magic or good luck.

All mandalas, everywhere, are part of the long series of sun symbols that began when early people first painted a sun circle on stone.

In most parts of the world the seasons influence people's feeling about the sun. Winter is a kind of death for the earth; spring is a joyful time of rebirth. But in tropical Africa near the Equator, as in the tropics anywhere, the sun's rays shine straight down all year round. Days and nights are of almost equal length. There is no real winter; there are only dry seasons and wet seasons.

People in Africa do not perform symbolic rites and ceremonies to bring back the warmth of the sun. There is no need; the warmth is always there. It is this warmth that makes the trees grow, and the crops people raise for food. The sun is a symbol of life on the African earth, but it can be destructive, too. People often suffer beneath this scorching heat.

Africans may speak of the sun in much the same words they use in speaking of God. The Akan of Ghana in West Africa call God "the Shining One." But though many Africans believe that God lives in the sky, or *is* the sky, this does not mean that to them the sun is the supreme God. Instead, the sun is often thought of as God's great gift to the world. God makes the sun to shine by day and the moon by night. In one story it is said that God created man so the sun would have someone for whom to shine.

The sun may be given a personal name in Africa, or even a temple, but few people worship it. Still, there are African myths about the sun, and occasionally it is considered a god, or referred to as if it were a god. In Dahomey it is said that Mawu, the moon, was twin of Lisa, the sun, a male god who lived in the east. Lisa was a fierce god; people suffered under his heat. Mawu was cool and gentle; people loved to tell stories and dance in her light. Mawu represented the wisdom of the world; Lisa its strength.

In the tropics the sun rises with great suddenness. All at once night is gone. Gone, too, say people of East Africa, are the evil spirits that walk in the darkness. To these people the moment in which light comes to the world is God. The sun itself is not God; only this sudden coming of light to the world.

Some of the signs that have represented the sun for countless ages are found in Africa, too. We have seen that early people in Africa painted sun wheels on rocks, and bronze objects made by the Ashanti of West Africa were often decorated with swastikas.

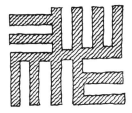

The Snake of Eternity is a well-known symbol in African art. The snake is curled in a circle, with its tail in its mouth, as if it were swallowing itself. It is painted on walls, worked in metal and wood, and woven into cloth. The snake-circle represents life beginning afresh and continuing without end. (The snake itself seems to start life over again

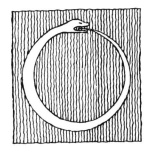

everytime it changes its skin.) This symbol is not now thought of as a sun symbol, but it probably had its origin in the earlier sun circles. In ancient Egypt it represented the path of the sun-god.

The sun itself in tropical Africa is born each day, day after day without end. The heat is relieved somewhat during the rainy seasons, and it is less intense in the highlands, but it is no wonder that this hot sun, important as it is, was not considered a god itself, but a gift of God that can either create or destroy.

VII. THE INCAS AND THE AZTECS

The Indians called Incas flourished in South America during the period of time that in Europe was called the Middle Ages. This lasted from the fall of the Roman Empire, in the fifth century A.D., to the late fifteenth century.

The Inca Empire stretched over two thousand miles along the Pacific coast of South America and east into the Andes Mountains. The Incas left no written records; they never developed any writing. We know a good deal about them, however, because other people wrote about them. Accounts of their civilization were recorded by Spaniards who came from Europe and conquered the Incas in the sixteenth century.

The illustration on the following page shows an Inca *quipu*. The knotted strings on a quipu are of various colors; they were used by the Incas for keeping accounts or records of things and events. This one was used as a calendar. Each string rep-

Inca quipu, used as a calendar.

resents a day of the year; all the strings together represent the rays of the sun. The circle is the sun itself and the curving line inside it indicates the movement of the sun throughout the year.

The Incas worshiped the sun and gave it the name Inti, which means light. The supreme ruler of the Incas, the Sapa Inca, was believed to be descended from the sun and was himself divine. When the Sapa Inca moved among the people he was the earthly representative of the sun passing among the stars.

Inti the sun descended into the ocean each evening. It was said that he swam all night in the waters under the earth; in the morning he appeared again in the sky, refreshed by his bath in the cool waters.

Inca villages were built in such a way that all the people could see the sun as it rose in the east. Together they saluted this sun, rejoicing in the light that brought life to the world.

The sun was celebrated by the Incas with feasts and festivals. The greatest of these was the Festival of the Sun, held at the time of the winter solstice, in June. (Since the land of the Incas lies south of the Equator, the seasons are the reverse of ours; their winter comes during our summer.)

Like winter festivals in other parts of the world, this one celebrated the lengthening of the days as the year turned toward spring. Once again the sun would become warmer and plants would grow in the earth. On the day of the solstice the Sapa Inca himself, the sun-king, led a procession of all the people of Cuzco, the city of the great Temple of the Sun. New fire, symbol of the light that was to come, was lit by focusing the rays of the sun on a mirror of burnished bronze and reflecting them onto a wad of cotton. A pure white llama was sacrificed to the sun and burned in this fire. The holy flame would be kept burning until three days before the next year's solstice.

Inca temples to the sun were probably more magnificent than those of any other nation in the world. Here, too, gold was the sacred metal of the sun. Nuggets of gold found upon the mountainsides were thought to be the sun's tears. The great Temple of the Sun at Cuzco was officially intended for Viracocha, the Inca god who had created the earth, the life on it, and all the other gods. But in practice it was the sun-god Inti who mattered, and gold was used lavishly in his honor.

The roof of the Temple of the Sun was made of precious timbers plated with gold. The doors were covered with gold and they opened to the east. Above the altar, on the western wall inside the temple, was a great golden disk with bright rays. This disk was embossed with a face to represent the sun and was studded with jewels. The rays of the rising sun fell upon the disk, filling the temple

*South American
Indian textile showing Inti,
the Inca sun-god.*

BRITISH MUSEUM, LONDON.

with a strange reflected light.

There were also humbler Inca symbols of the sun-god. The giant sunflower was once one of these. Its seeds were eaten in certain religious ceremonies. The Maidens of the Sun, Inca priestesses, wore on their breasts big sunflower blossoms made of gold, bright disks of the sun. The Spanish conquerors especially coveted these sunflower disks.

The sun-king and his officials controlled every aspect of the lives of the Inca people. The sun-king was considered the owner of all the land, and it was cultivated as he directed. Even though the people had little freedom, there was usually enough food for everyone and the system seems to have worked well. Then the Spaniards came and the whole intricate structure of Inca society and sun worship was destroyed.

Unfortunately, very little artistic evidence of the sun worship of the Incas remains. Here and there a sculptured vase or other object may portray the sun-god. The quipu and the chibcha textile in the illustrations are rare surviving examples of Inca sun symbolism.

The Spaniards brought Christianity to the vanquished Incas, and their religion became a mixture of Christian and earlier pagan beliefs. The new Christian God was often identified with the sun-god of former times.

Even today, in Cuzco, high in the Andes Mountains, people hold a week-long ceremony each year in honor of the sun. There is a pageant beginning with an ancient salute to the sun. A llama is sacrificed; chants are sung. Then everyone dances. This is now partly a Christian ceremony, but it has its roots in the ages-old Inca festival to the sun-god.

We must depend on Spanish conquerors also for our knowledge of the Aztecs, the Indians who controlled most of Mexico when the Spaniards arrived there in the year 1519. The Aztecs, unlike the Incas, did have writing, but the Spaniards, convinced that anything they could not understand was somehow unholy, destroyed most of the Aztec documents.

Many gods were important to the Aztecs, but the sun-god had a special place in their worship. They considered themselves his chosen people, yet to them the sun was often a dark symbol of destruction. They knew that the permanent disappearance of the sun would mean death to everything on earth, and they were possessed by a terrible fear that this might happen. Each sunset seemed like a failure of the spark of life, a kind of failure also in themselves.

The sun-god was called Tezcatlipoca, or "smoking mirror," though he had other names for various aspects of his behavior. He was supposed to be invisible, but he might sometimes appear as a passing shadow, a frightful monster, or a dim giant that moved through the night.

The sun-god had to battle each night with the many gods of darkness. Each night he died in this struggle; at dawn he was born again. In some Aztec paintings the sun-god is shown as a skeleton at sunrise. The Aztecs believed that he could be restored only with human blood. Each year a handsome young man who had been captured in battle was chosen to personify the sun. For a full year he was given special honors, fine clothes, and four lovely girls to wait on him. He was taught to play sacred music on the flute. Everywhere he went people worshiped him and kissed the ground where he walked.

Then came the end. The captive was led outside the city in a solemn procession. At the great pyramid of the Sun Temple he mounted the steps slowly, just as the sun slowly mounts the sky. At the top, a priest opened the young man's breast with a single thrust of the knife and raised his heart, still beating, to the sun.

The victim was not pitied. Indeed, he was assured of a happy future in heaven. It was believed that his spirit would become one of the eagles who lifted the sun from the darkness of night and brought it out into the dawn. But to us it seems horrible that the Aztec priests could perform such tortures.

This victim was not the only one to be sacrificed by the Aztecs. They believed that a constant flow of blood was needed to sustain the gods. Thousands of people, most of them prisoners of war, were sacrificed to the sun each year. Each victim was first painted yellow.

Aztec drawing showing heart being removed from a victim.

Victims were offered also to many other gods. The Aztecs believed that the gods had used their own blood in the creation of humankind by mixing it with the bones of men of earlier times. People must, therefore, in turn, give blood to nourish the gods. If this was not done, the life-giving grain might not grow and the sun-god might not be reborn after his long struggle in the night.

The Aztecs had other ways of pleasing the sun-god. For one thing, there were ball games. These were held on holy ground close to the temples.

Aztec ball game and ball court.

A typical ball court had the shape of a rather squat letter H. High, thick walls enclosed it; people could watch the game from the top. Heavy stone rings were set high in a wall at the center of the court. Players would try to knock a rubber ball through the hole in these rings without touching the ball with their hands or feet. It could be struck with thigh or knee, head or shoulder. Each flight of the ball represented the journey of the sun across the sky.

The temples of the Aztecs, built at the top of high pyramids, were themselves symbols of the sun. There, high above the ground, the worshiper would be closer to the sun and the other gods. The pyramids were made of rough earth covered with cut stone. Four sides sloped upward toward the center. This form gives one a feeling of motion, up, up toward the sky. One side, or sometimes more than one, of the pyramid had steps leading to the temple at the top. The pyramid shown in the picture stood in the ancient Aztec capital, Tenochtitlán (now Mexico City). It had 360 steps, one for each of the 360 days of the Aztec calendar. These steps symbolize the journey of the sun, day by day throughout the year.

The famous Aztec sunstone shown on the following page is still another symbol of the sun. The face of the sun-god is at the center of this huge stone disk that measures more than twelve feet across. In the next circle the hands of the sun-god, sharp with eagle claws, are seen squeezing human hearts. Four suns of previous times are shown in four squares within the same circle. Next is a circle containing the twenty pictured day signs used to represent the days of the month in the Aztec calendar. Rays of the sun, and jewels, surround this. Finally, two fire serpents encircle the whole design, their heads facing each other at the bottom. It was partly because of these serpents that the sun-god could conquer his enemies and day could follow night, over and over again, year after year.

The sun-god had many faces, but none as violent and bloody as that envisioned by the Aztecs of Mexico.

Aztec sunstone, from Symbols, Signs and Signets *by Ernest Lehner; Dover.*

VIII. THE INDIANS AND
ESKIMOS OF NORTH AMERICA

The dawning of the sun, though it happens every day, is "a thing very mysterious." So said a Pawnee Indian of the North American prairie. The Indians of the prairie often greeted the rising sun with raised palms, a prayer for strength in the coming day, and a pipe of peace.

The smoke of the pipe might be directed first to the east, then to the south, west, and north, as the sun moves. These four directions were connected by an imaginary line marking the circle of the horizon. This was one circle of the day. Another circle was made by the path of the sun itself through the sky from dawn to dusk and its journey at night beneath the world. This was the prairie Indians' Wheel of Day.

In this timeless wheel, the sun of morning brought life; the sun of full day was the sun of brave deeds and of seeing the world clearly; the sun at dusk was the sun of quiet thought. At night

WATER COLOR, 1907/BETTMAN ARCHIVE, NEW YORK.

*A Plains Indian mother holds her baby up
to be blessed by the rising sun.*

the sun journeyed through the caverns of the dead until finally it was born again at dawn.

The prairie Indians played a game in which a wheel represented the course of the sun; darts were thrown at it. Often this wheel was divided into four sections, for the four points of daily time: morning, noon, evening, and night.

Everywhere in North America the sun was one of the chief gods. The religion of the Indian tribes varied greatly, however. To some the sun was the Supreme God. To others he was less important than the Great Spirit who created heaven and earth. Usually the sun was considered a god rather than a goddess.

Some Indian tribes lived by hunting wild animals and gathering nuts, seeds, and roots. As in other parts of the world, these hunting people were less dependent on the yearly course of the sun than were the planting people. Those who raised food in their own gardens had to watch the sun all through the year. Seedtime and harvest, life and death, depended on the sun. So powerful a force must indeed be a god.

The religion of the Indians was expressed in two principal ways—in myths and in rituals. The Indians were great storytellers. In their myths they told about their understanding of the world and the beginnings of life on earth. Certain kinds of myths were repeated over and over again, varying sometimes only a little from tribe to tribe. Sun myths are numerous. It is clear that to the Indians, as to many other people, the sun was a symbol of light and life.

A sun myth told in the Northwest reminds us of the ancient Greek story of the unfortunate Phaëthon, son of Helios. In the Indian tale an animal, the mink, is permitted to carry the sun disk across the sky. Like Phaëthon, the mink is inexperienced, he travels too close to earth, and there is terrible burning.

There are varied Indian stories of the creation of the sun. The tribes of the Northwest believed that the raven, their Supreme God, found the sun one day by accident. He realized how important such a light would be for mankind, so he set the sun in the heavens, and there it remained.

In many myths the sun is first placed in the sky too close to the earth, making everything much too hot. A Cherokee story tells us that the animals set the sun in an east–west track just overhead, so that the world need no longer be dark. But it was blazing hot that way. Crawfish had his shell scorched a bright red; his meat was spoiled and the Cherokees would not eat it. Conjurers then put the sun in a slightly higher track. It was still too hot. The sun was raised again and again until finally, the seventh time, it was just under the arch of the sky, and this was right.

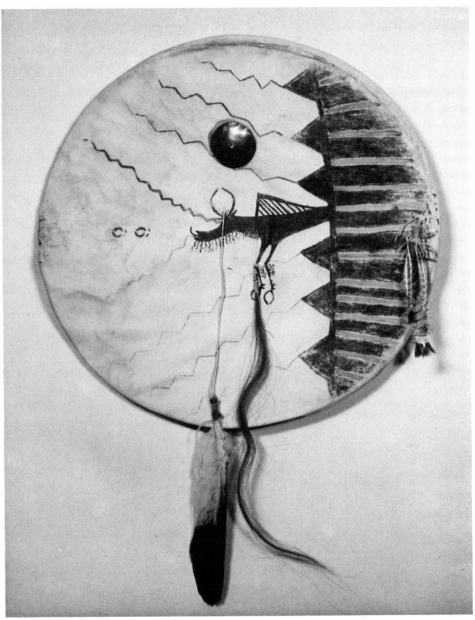

Shield with painting of deer and sun. Crow Indians, Montana.

The Indians of the Southwest tell a number of stories about the origin of the sun. In a Navajo story, the people of early times lived in a sort of twilight. Wanting more light, several tribes met to decide what to do. They concluded that a sun, a moon, and stars should be placed above the earth to give light. First the sky itself had to be created. Then the old men of the Navajo made the sun in a house specially built for the purpose. Two mute flute players were chosen to carry the sun and the moon on their shoulders. They staggered under the weight. The one who carried the sun bent so low that it almost burned up the earth. The old men of the tribe then lit their pipes and puffed smoke hard at the sun. This made it move higher in the heavens. Four times they had to do this to keep the sun from burning up the world.

The flutist who carried the sun was known as a Sun-Carrier. The idea of a carrier was a common one in the Southwest. The Navajo Sun-Carrier was named Tshohanoai, and it was believed that the sun could not cross the sky each day without him.

As he moved westward, the Sun-Carrier sang:

In my thoughts I approach,
The Sun-God approaches,
Earth's end he approaches. . . .
In old age walking the beautiful trail.

At the end of the day's journey Tshohanoai removed the blazing disk of the sun from his back and hung it on a peg on the west wall of his lodge. There the disk shook and clanged for some time, going "tla, tla, tla, tla."

Many Indian myths tell of the adventures of a hero or heroic brothers whose father is the sun. The boys often had to go through a series of terrible ordeals, from which they were saved only by magic, in order to prove that they were indeed children of the sun.

The rites and ceremonies that are a part of the Indian religion tell us even more about their feeling for the sun than do the myths. The rituals are a symbolic way of expressing the Indian understanding of life.

When the Indians of the prairie greeted the rising sun with a prayer and a pipe of peace, this was a ritual. The sun had a part also in many of the rites and ceremonies of the planting Indians, even when it was not thought of as the Supreme God. Ceremonies were needed when the year turned toward winter, to keep the sun from disappearing entirely as the days grew shorter. Other ceremonies helped to give the sun strength when spring came, when seeds were planted, and in the long days of summer when a hot sun was needed to ripen the corn.

The Natchez were planting Indians who lived in the forests and fields in the southern part of the United States, near the present city of Natchez, Mississippi. Like other Indians of North America, their chief crop was maize, which we call corn. These Indians shared many customs with the Aztecs farther south. This is not really surprising. Travelers, traders, and conquerors had moved north from Mexico into various parts of North America. They brought news of the people to the south, of their daily lives, their celebrations, their worship of the gods. Some Indians listened and continued with their old ways. But the Natchez evidently took over some of the Aztec customs.

Model of a Natchez Indian village in early times. The sun-king is being carried on a litter; in the background is the temple.

AMERICAN MUSEUM OF
NATURAL HISTORY, NEW YORK

These Indians had a king who had absolute power over the people; no other tribe north of Mexico had this. The king was called "The Sun," and the people believed he was descended from the sun-god. (In this respect the Natchez resembled the Incas of South America.) The king wore a crown and a beautiful cloak, both made of feathers. He was so sacred that he was not allowed to dirty his feet by walking on ordinary ground. Indians who had volunteered to serve him carried him about in a litter. These servants asked to be killed when "The Sun" died, so that they could accompany him in his afterlife. The common people were thought to have no afterlife at all.

The Natchez worshiped the sun itself above all. They built for it a wooden temple on a great mound; at each end of the temple roof was placed a carved eagle, bird of the sun. Inside this temple the Indians kept an undying fire, symbol of the sun. The two guards who watched the fire would be killed if they let it go out.

Sometimes the Natchez sacrificed a prisoner of war to the sun by tying him to a wooden frame and shooting arrows into him. But they never indulged in mass executions as did the Aztecs.

Another activity of the Natchez that probably came from the Aztecs was the ceremonial ball game. Their ball was stuffed with moss and cov-

ered with deerskin; it was about as big as a fist. The ball was to be hit with the hands; it must not be held or allowed to fall to the ground. The players, sometimes hundreds of them, would try to bat the ball in this way against the walls of a cabin built by their own side.

The ball game was part of a ceremony of thanksgiving held by the Natchez each year before they ate the first ripe corn. The sun-king was carried to the ceremony in his litter, but he took part in the game as head of one side. Similar ball games were played all through eastern North America.

The greatest festival of the Plains Indians was the ritual generally known as the Sun Dance. The Dakotas, as the Sioux Indians called themselves, named this the "Gazing-at-the-Sun Dance," but it was given different names by other tribes. For all of the tribes the purpose of the ritual was to help people feel close to the earth, to the sun that warms it, and to all the spirits in the world. If this was done, surely good health would be theirs, and many children; the buffalo would increase and provide abundant food.

The Plains Indians lived mainly by hunting the buffalo for its meat, but the buffalo was more than a source of food. Blankets, tepee coverings, ropes, tools, and craft materials—almost everything the Indians used came from the hide, tendons, horns,

Photos in margins: Beaded blanket bands of the Dakota Indians, with sun wheel patterns.

and fat of the buffalo. A ritual that concerned the welfare of all the people had to take the buffalo into account. But since the sun was, after all, the source of all life, prayers to the sun and symbols of the sun were an essential part of the ritual.

The festival was held every year at midsummer, at a time when plants were green on the plains and the buffalo were abundant. Among the Dakotas there were four days of preparation for the final ceremony. These days began with an offering of smoke to the rising sun. Like incense, smoke from a sacred pipe was blown to the sky above. The four days of preparation closed with an offering of smoke to the setting sun. Those who were to take part in the ceremony then gathered on high ground and prayed to the Four Winds and to the Spirit Above for bright blue days for the ceremony. As the sun sank out of sight, the mouthpiece of the pipe was held up to it. We ask your blessing, the people prayed.

The rest of the festival occupied four more days. There were processions and gatherings, a buffalo feast and dance, and offerings of smoke. A great cottonwood tree, straight and strong, was chosen, cut down, stripped of bark, and set up in the camp. This was the Sun Pole; the final Sun Dance would take place around it. The pole was painted with four vertical stripes—red for the West, blue for the North, green for the East, and

yellow for the South. Symbolic objects were bound to the pole, among them buffalo hair and the red banner of the sun.

On the fourth and final day the Buffalo Dance came first and was repeated four times. Then, at last, came the Gazing-at-the-Sun Dance. It was performed by warriors who had made a vow to take part in this dance in return for help given by the spirits or by the sun in time of trouble.

In some tribes, including the Dakota, the warriors were attached to the Sun Pole by ropes fastened to skewers inserted under the muscles of back or chest. All day they fixed their eyes on the sun and slowly, on their toes or on the balls of their feet, they circled the sacred pole. Drums beat. People sang songs of encouragement to the warriors.

At last the flesh would be torn and the warrior would be free of his bonds. Songs of victory and rejoicing would greet this accomplishment. In this way a warrior felt that he was giving to the sun, or to the Great Spirit, part of his own body, the thing that was most truly his. Often a warrior had a great dream or vision, either during the dance or sometime afterward. The dream would be proof that the spirits of nature, the sun, and the Great Spirit himself, looked favorably on the warrior's part in the Gazing-at-the-Sun Dance.

This self-torture was not practiced by all the

tribes, however. Some forbade the shedding of blood during the ceremony.

The Sun Dance was a kind of prayer, a thanksgiving in which all the people felt their closeness to the sun that brought them life. One chief directing this ceremony prayed:

Great Sun Power! I am praying for my people that they may be happy in the summer and that they may live through the cold of winter. . . . Great Spirit! bless our children, friends, and visitors through a happy life. May our trails lie straight and level before us. Let us live to be old. We are all your children and ask these things with good hearts.

The Pueblo Indians of the American Southwest believe that Father Sun and Mother Earth are the greatest gods of all. These gods are known by many different names; the sun is sometimes called Heart of the Sky.

Pueblo Indians often sit on the flat roofs of their houses, hour after hour, contemplating the sun as it rises in the clear blue sky.

The sun plays an important part in many of the ceremonies and dances of the Pueblo people, who live primarily by growing corn. The sun-priest guides the ceremonial life of the people, as the sun itself guides them through the yearly cycle of planting, growth, and harvest. The disk of the sun is seen in rituals and in the art of the Pueblo almost as frequently as it was in ancient Egypt. In the Flute Ceremony a great disk encircled by eagle feathers and streamers is carried high. It is an emblem of the sun.

In sign writing, and in weaving, pottery making, bead work, and sand paintings, North American Indians represent the sun in a number of ways. A few examples are shown here:

On facing page:
Navajo sun painting,
made with sand, then reproduced
on cloth. By a medicine
man in Arizona, about 1905–1912.

Below:
Apache tray basket with sun design.
AMERICAN MUSEUM OF
NATURAL HISTORY, NEW YORK.

SMITHSONIAN INSTITUTION, BUREAU OF AMERICAN ETHNOLOGY, WASHINGTON, D.C.

The swastika was often used as a decoration on Indian pottery, baskets, and blankets. The Indian swastika had its arms pointing counterclockwise, and it meant good luck.

Papago tray basket with elaborated swastika design, Arizona.

AMERICAN MUSEUM
OF NATURAL HISTORY,
NEW YORK.

*Navajo rug
with swastika
design.*

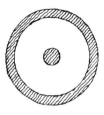

The ancient Egyptian sign for the sun is known to the North American Indians, too, but to them it means *spirit*. Perhaps, even so, the people's experience with the sun as spirit helped to make this sign, seen at the left.

To the Indians, animals are often symbols. The sun may appear as a porcupine with beautiful quills, or a mink, or a redheaded woodpecker.

The sun has quite a different meaning for the Eskimos in the far North. These are hunting people. For them there is no yearly cycle of the growth of plants from seed to harvest. As in the Scandinavian countries, there is a great difference in the length of the days at different seasons. When the days grow shorter and shorter in the autumn, the sun itself seems to be disappearing. Eskimos may then make a net of string between their hands, for magic, to catch the sun so it cannot go away so soon. When at last the days begin to grow longer, they will play "cup and ball." The ball is a symbol of the sun. Catch it in a cup; then surely the days will continue to grow longer.

The Wheel of Day follows its path day by day. The Indians and the Eskimos know the power of the mysterious sun that makes this path. Life and death are brought by the sun to everyone, and this, they said, shall be forever.

IX. THE MAGICAL SUN

P eople have expressed their feelings about the sun in many ways. They have not merely worshiped the great sun in the sky as a symbol of light. Nor have they always looked to their religious leaders to interpret the meaning of the sun in human life. Instead, they have thought up their own ways of using magic to make the sun behave or to prevent it from doing harm. Amazing superstitions about the sun have grown up.

We have seen how the Eskimos of North America make a net of string in the fall to keep the sun from going away. This is only one example of the magic that people thought could influence the sun.

In Scotland it was believed that walking around a person "sunwise," in the direction of the sun's motion, would bring him good luck. To circle in the opposite direction brought evil. Similar beliefs have been found in other countries.

In parts of Germany, on Saint John's Day, hunters would fire at the sun in the early morning. This they thought would bring them good luck in the chase. On the other hand, the opposite of this belief was found elsewhere in Germany, where it was said that whoever fired toward the sun on Saint John's Day would be condemned to hunt forever after, all his days and all his nights.

Certain European superstitions about the sun were connected with Christian customs:

If women danced in the sun on Candlemas Day (February 2), the flax would grow well that year.

The sun had to shine at least for a short time every Sunday, so that the Blessed Virgin could dry her veil.

On Good Friday the sun grieved because of the crucifixion of Christ and would not shine until three o'clock in the afternoon.

Three Saturdays in the year, when the Virgin Mary mourned for her son, the sun would not shine at all.

We now know that dreaming about the sun means very different things to different people. But in earlier times certain definite things were thought to be meant by such dreams. We read in an old Dream Book:

To dream you see the sun rise means that your sweetheart will be faithful and you will have good news from friends.

To dream you see the sun set means that your sweetheart will be unfaithful and you will have bad news.

To dream you see the sun shine means that you will be successful as a lover and wealth will be yours.

To dream of the sun behind a cloud means that you will meet with many hardships and great danger.

Sun of Sunday, from an old Gypsy Planet and Dream Book.

Other groups of people have used sun symbols in their own way. In the Middle Ages the alchemists experimented continually, attempting to turn mercury and other substances into gold. A mysterious substance called the philosopher's stone was supposed to help accomplish this. To keep their work secret, the alchemists invented special symbols. The secrets were so well kept that the meaning of some of these symbols is unknown to us even today.

An alchemist of the sixteenth century.
The sun is at his window;
beside him stands Leo the lion,
astrologer's symbol of the sun.

The alchemists associated a metal with each planet: lead for Saturn, silver for the moon, gold for the sun because gold is the most valuable of metals and was considered the final aim of nature. To the left is the alchemists' sign for the sun. (You may remember this same sign as the Egyptian hieroglyph for sun.)

Alchemists sought to discover the laws of nature and use them in their work. Their symbols expressed this search; they were not just for magic. The symbols had, besides, a religious meaning. They may have been an expression of dreams, of the alchemists' attempts to understand the meaning of their own lives. Illustrations in the books of the alchemists are full of astonishing figures of the sun and the planets.

Astrologers use symbols also, but for a different purpose from that of the alchemists. Astrological symbols are employed in predicting the influence of the stars on human affairs.

Astrologers believe that the sun passes through a different constellation of stars every thirty days in the year. The twelve constellations have signs known as signs of the zodiac. Astrologers say that a person's life is influenced by the sign under which he or she was born. The sign of Leo, the lion, in the last third of July and the first two-thirds of August, is governed by the sun itself. Leo is a fiery sign; orange is its color, and the metal as-

*A glass zodiac with sun in the
center, made by Glass Masters, New York,
designed from medieval woodcuts.*

sociated with it is gold. Just so, the alchemists associated gold with the sun. To the astrologers the sun is a symbol of power and good fortune.

Tarot card number nineteen: The Sun.

A golden sun disk with a face and many rays appears on the "sun card" in the "Tarot" deck of cards. Tarot cards are used in parts of Europe and the United States for playing a game and also for fortune telling and gambling. But it is believed that they once had a deeper meaning. Students would study a card until the symbol on it seemed to become a part of themselves. By concentrating on a visible symbol they might come to understand thoughts and feelings that could not be seen. Little is actually known, however, about this use of the cards. Perhaps the bright sun on a Tarot card represented the light people feel in themselves.

People took their magic seriously; they were sure it worked. Many people today believe in the power of the sun in astrology. But in earlier times, before there were scientific explanations, the greatest magic of all seemed to be the sun itself, bright light in the sky that never failed.

X. FROM MYTHOLOGY TO SCIENCE

In early times people had only one way of learning about the sun. They watched it with their own two eyes and observed its changing behavior from season to season. This sun, they decided, was a glowing disk of fire, much smaller than the vast world on which they lived. They could see how small it was. It could be hidden by just the tip of a finger held at arm's length.

People saw the sun rise each day above the horizon in the east. Steadily it moved up the sky until it was at its highest point at noon. Then it moved just as steadily down the sky to the west, where it disappeared below the horizon. The earth itself, meanwhile, did not seem to move at all.

In ancient times it was widely believed that at night the sun sank into a vast ocean with a hissing sound. After all, why should it not hiss— a thing so fiery hot meeting the cool water of an ocean? All night the sun sailed across this ocean toward the eastern horizon.

As we have seen, people worshiped the sun as a god. They invented a complicated and wonderful mythology to explain its daily rising and setting, its changing aspects as the year progressed. Sun worshipers built observatories where they could watch the heavens and feel closer to their god. Astrologers studied the skies for signs that would help them to understand the affairs of men and predict the future. All these things in time led to a certain amount of actual knowledge about the sun, the moon, and the stars. Imaginative guesses sometimes proved later to be true.

Astrology was an important business in ancient Mesopotamia, though it was at first reserved for the use of kings and for determining what would happen to the state. The astrologers of Mesopotamia learned to distinguish the stars from the planets. They studied the path of the sun through the sky from day to day and worked out an elaborate system for recording the passage of time.

Several interesting scientific instruments were produced by these astrologers. One was a kind of sundial called a *gnomon,* a stone column placed in the soil on level ground. When its shadow was shortest during the day, the time was noon. Its shortest shadow of the year marked the summer solstice, when the sun was highest in the sky and the day was longest.

The Mesopotamian astrologers mixed predictions and wild guesses with their knowledge. It was still believed that the earth was the center of the universe. Nevertheless we can say that these astrologers were to some extent astronomers. They tried to use their human reason to understand the sun, the moon, and the stars.

The Egyptians believed that the universe was much the same shape as their own country. It was, they thought, a long valley surrounded by moun-

Diagram of the Egyptian conception of the universe.

tains, running north and south. Egypt was at the center of this valley. The sky was a sort of metallic cover, supported by mountain peaks. Stars hung from this cover on the ends of cords; night after night they were miraculously lit. In the illustration on the previous page we see the sun-god Ra about to set out in his boat on his daily journey across the valley.

Egyptian astronomers studied the sky for purely practical reasons. They wanted to know the best day and hour for religious ceremonies. They also needed to predict the time when the River Nile would flood the fields, and this required a knowledge of the seasons. For these purposes they made maps of the heavens and identified the principal stars. But they did not really add much to the science of astronomy; knowledge for its own sake did not interest them.

The philosophers of ancient Greece, on the other hand, were very much interested in finding out about the universe. Ionia, a region in Asia Minor that was colonized by the Greeks, has been called the cradle of the modern scientific spirit. Still, much of the scientific theory of the time was guesswork. There were no instruments for watching and understanding the skies, no telescope to magnify the heavenly bodies. "Facts" were invented to suit a scholar's favorite theories, and they were usually quite wrong.

The story of early Greek astronomy is a fascinating one, but here we are concerned mainly with theories about the sun. We find that the sun as fact and the sun as symbol were often greatly confused.

The size of the sun was a subject for endless speculation. The Greek philosopher Heraclitus had a definite answer to this question. The sun, he said, is just the size of a human foot, and its light has to be rekindled every day.

Anaxagoras, on the other hand, described the sun as a mass of constantly burning metal, bigger than the Peloponnesus, the peninsula that formed the southern part of Greece. He was of course more nearly right than Heraclitus, but the priests of Athens, the city where he lived, were horrified. What? The sun was not a god? This was blasphemy; surely a crime. Anaxagoras was put on trial and was barely acquitted. He was forced to leave Athens.

The Greek astronomer Aristarchus of Samos in the third century B.C. made one of the most important discoveries of all. He was the first man we know of who claimed that the earth travels around the sun. The fixed stars and the sun stand still, he said, while the earth, rotating on its own axis, circles the sun once in a year. He also figured that the sun must be three hundred times the size of the earth.

*Ptolemy's conception
of the universe. The earth
is at the center with
the sun revolving around it.
From an old atlas.*

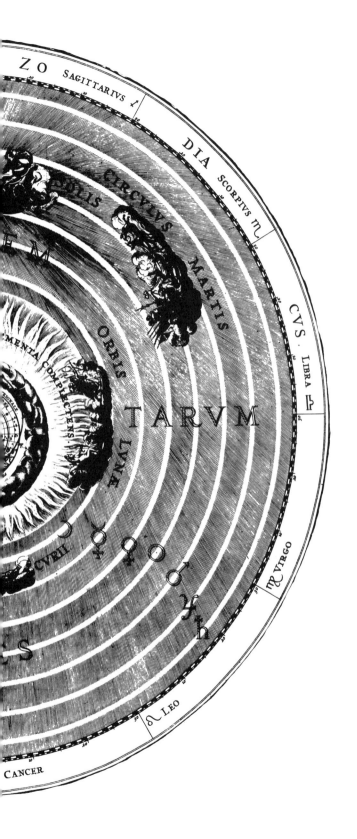

Aristarchus's ideas, though based on careful observation, were highly unpopular. People simply could not bear to think that their earth was not the center of the universe. It made them feel so much less important. As a result, Aristarchus's findings were ignored.

At about this time guesswork in astronomy was largely given up in favor of exact observation and mathematical calculation. The sun as symbol did not lose its importance, but it was less often confused with the sun as fact.

The Greek astronomer, Hipparchus, working in the latter half of the second century B.C., added more to the knowledge of astronomy than any other thinker of ancient times. He lived in Rhodes, thought to be the birthplace of the sun-god Helios. Among other things, Hipparchus made the first catalogue of the stars and figured out the size of the moon and its distance from the earth. He knew more about the sun and the earth than most people do today. In spite of this, however, he rejected Aristarchus's idea that the earth travels around the sun. Instead, he went back to the older idea that the sun and the planets move around the earth.

Two and a half centuries later, Ptolemy, a Greek living in Alexandria in Egypt, perfected Hipparchus's plan of the universe and wrote a great book summarizing the work of earlier astronomers.

He, too, though, believed that the earth was the center of the universe.

To be sure, the motions of the sun, the moon, and the planets, as he observed them, did not always fit in with this theory. This did not bother Ptolemy. He thought up clever explanations for what he saw. This shows how far the human mind can go in inventing reasons for what it wants to believe.

For more than twelve centuries Ptolemy's picture of an earth-centered universe was accepted by most astronomers. It was completely false.

The ancient Romans did not produce a single important astronomer. Nothing new was learned about the sky, either, during all of the medieval period in Europe. People returned to thinking the earth was flat. The sun as symbol was not forgotten; quite pagan sunbursts appeared in Christian churches, and much of the sun lore of ancient times persisted among the people. But few seemed to want to understand how the sun brought the day and the changing seasons.

Gradually new ideas began stirring among the scientists. Leonardo da Vinci wrote in one of his notebooks: "The sun does not move." A real break with medieval indifference was then made by the Polish mathematician, Nicolaus Copernicus. He studied the astronomy of the Greeks and was especially impressed with Aristarchus's claim that

*A medieval seeker after
knowledge pokes his head through
the sky to observe the
mechanics of space. Old woodcut.*

the earth travels around the sun. Ptolemy's elaborate "proofs" that the earth is the center of the universe did not make sense to him.

For many years Copernicus observed the skies and worked out the orbits of the planets by mathematics. He was the first person to believe that all the planets, including the earth, revolve around the sun. The earth, he said, turns on its own axis every twenty-four hours and travels around the sun every year.

Copernicus could not actually prove this because he lacked the precise instruments that as-

tronomers use today. There was as yet no telescope. But it was clear to him that his system
explained the motions of the heavenly bodies in
a much simpler and more logical way than did
the system of Ptolemy.

Copernicus hesitated to publish his findings. The
authorities of the church still insisted that the
earth must be the center of the universe. They
were likely to punish anyone who thought otherwise. But at last Copernicus's great book, *On the
Revolutions of the Heavenly Spheres,* was pub-
lished in 1543, the year of his death. The book
was science, but it was mythology and poetry,
too. Copernicus wrote of the sun:

*He is rightly called the Lamp, the Mind, the
Ruler of the Universe. . . . The Sun sits upon a
royal throne ruling his children the planets which
circle around him.*

It was a hundred years before Copernicus's system entirely replaced that of Ptolemy. But a great
change was already occurring in the way people
thought about their world. Some, at least, were
beginning to have faith in the power of human
reason to explain the world in ways that could
not be perceived by their senses. This made it
possible to believe that the solid earth, turning

Copernicus's conception of the universe. The sun is at the center and the earth, an important planet, moves around it. From an old atlas.

all the time, moved around the sun, even though it was the sun that appeared to move.

In 1973, five hundred years after the birth of Copernicus, the United States issued a commemorative postage stamp in his honor. On it appears a portrait of Copernicus holding an instrument that demonstrates his theory. In its center is a golden sunburst.

The Italian scientist Galileo called himself "the first observer of marvelous things!" In the year 1609 he heard of the invention of the telescope in the Netherlands. He saw its possibilities at once and set to work to build his own. His telescope had a magnifying power of thirty times.

Galileo first observed the mountains and the craters of the moon; no one had ever seen them before. With great excitement he turned his telescope on the planets. Next he discovered darker spots on the face of the sun. The spots appeared to move across the disk, and this proved that the sun, though it did not move in an orbit, like the earth and the planets, did spin on its own axis. "It really *does* move!"

Galileo's findings were at first very popular. But some of the other Italian scientists were afraid of these new ideas. They decided that the telescope must be the work of the devil. The church forbade Galileo to continue his teaching, saying that it was contrary to Holy Scripture. At last, old and unwell, Galileo was put on trial and threatened with torture. This was too much; the weary scientist read aloud to his accusers a denial of all he held to be true.

But the truth will come out, and little by little, important knowledge was added to the science of astronomy. Scientists now know that the sun is not solid, like the earth. It is a burning mass, consisting partly of gases, including hydrogen and helium, and various metals, among them iron and magnesium. The heat of the sun is so intense that even its metals are in the form of gases. The temperature at the sun's surface is about 11,000 degrees Fahrenheit. Inside, it is probably millions of degrees. (Here on earth, water boils at a mere 212 degrees Fahrenheit, and we think that is hot!) Anaxagoras was partly right when he described the sun as a mass of constantly burning metal.

We know more, now, about sunspots; they are violent storms over the surface of the sun. And we know something about the sun's size; the sun is so big that it would take more than a million earths to make anything that size. Aristarchus, who had figured that the sun was three hundred times the size of the earth, would have been amazed.

Much has been learned, too, of the ways in which sunlight brings life to the world. One of the most fascinating is the process called photo-

BETTMAN ARCHIVE, NEW YORK.

Galileo at work.

synthesis, by which green leaves use the energy in sunlight to make food for plants, combining the carbon dioxide in the air with water.

And, at last, men have even seen with their own eyes that the earth is round. Astronauts have stood on the surface of the moon and watched our earth high overhead, a small sphere in the vastness of space. This earth, to be sure, is not the center of the universe. Instead, the astronauts see it as a little oasis in space, warmed by the sun. Our earth is the only planet that is covered with living things, the only place we know where people can live. We can think of that when the sun seems to climb the sky in the east, bringing another day.

We have been speaking only of sun science in Europe, and indeed, the discoveries of European scientists have had the greatest influence on astronomy as we know it today. But people in other parts of the world were also studying the heavens. The Chinese, using only the naked eye, had observed sunspots before these were known to Galileo. They could also predict a solar eclipse, the darkening of the sun when the moon passes between it and the earth.

The Hindus in ancient India considered the sun the great clock of the world, and they studied its movements carefully. A number of their religious writings were called *Surya Pannatti,* which means "comprehension of the sun." Astronomy as a science did not go far in India, however. The astronomers felt they must make their observations conform to Hindu religious beliefs. It was considered more important to write poetic thoughts about the sun than to record actual observations. In the ancient Hindu view of the universe everything was double—there were two suns, two moons, and two complete systems of stars.

The Aztecs and Mayas of Mexico were also concerned with astronomy mainly for religious reasons. Nevertheless, they seem to have observed the heavens with considerable accuracy. Experts who have studied the great Aztec sunstone tell us that these people had a knowledge of astronomy and knew how long the earth took to revolve around the sun.

A tower discovered among ruins of the Mayan city of Chichén Itzá is a real observatory. Small openings in its thick walls were used for study of the sun, the moon, and the stars. From these observations the Mayas worked out a remarkably accurate calendar.

People have told time by the sun for thousands of years. The simplest way was simply by calling it morning when the sun rose, noon when it was overhead, and evening when it set. But in quite

Ruins of the Mayan observatory at Chichén Itzá.

early times people wanted to tell time more precisely than that.

We have seen that astrologers in Mesopotamia used the shadow of a vertical stone column called a gnomon for telling time. The ancient Chinese also had a gnomon. They observed that the shadow of the gnomon at noon, its shortest of the day, changed in length from day to day. From this they were able to make certain astronomical calculations.

It is thought that the obelisks of the Egyptians were used, like gnomons, for determining noontime. The Greeks probably borrowed the idea of the gnomon from the Mesopotamians.

In ancient times the day was divided into hours in a way that seems strange to us. The hours of daylight were divided into twelve equal parts; the night was also divided into twelve parts. Since day and night are not usually equally long, the lengths of the hours differed. The lengths of the hours also changed with the seasons, as the days grew shorter or longer. This system made it possible to measure time, at least in a general way, with a gnomon.

Finally, in the Middle Ages, our present system of unchanging hours was adopted. Another kind of sundial then came into general use. It consisted of a flat surface with a slanting metal bar projecting from it. This is the sundial we most often see today. The metal bar is called, appropriately, a gnomon, or *style*. As the sun appears to move across the sky, the shadow of the gnomon on the dial moves. Markings on the dial indicate the hour. (This differs from the earlier gnomon, which depended on the length of its shadow rather than on its position.) The astronomers of Mesopotamia had a sundial of this kind, as well as their gnomon. The Arabs perfected its design at an early date.

Most sundials do not tell time very accurately. After all, the position of the shadow cast by the gnomon from hour to hour varies with the seasons, as the path of the sun varies. Our clocks and watches give us more exact measurement of time.

Sundial in a garden.

SUNDIALS, NEW IPSWICH, NEW HAMPSHIRE.

But sundials can be highly decorative, and are often found on public buildings and in gardens.

In Europe vertical sundials are sometimes placed on the south wall of buildings. The horizontal sundial is the kind most often found in gardens. The gnomon is set at its center. It takes an astronomer to construct an accurate vertical or horizontal sundial. Complicated mathematical calculations must be made. In the northern hemisphere the gnomon must point toward the North Pole; in the southern hemisphere, toward the South Pole. The slant of the gnomon must be the same as the slant of the earth's axis.

Today it seems that the sun as symbol has really been separated from the sun as fact. The god of the sun is dead. But is this really true?

Our modern sun worshipers do not call the sun a god. Nevertheless they flock to the beaches in summer and lie beneath the hot sun while they watch their skin darken or grow red and sore. When at last this seems too much, they sit beneath huge circular umbrellas that are surely sun wheels. These people indeed, like earlier worshipers, are prepared to make sacrifices to the sun.

Many who have the time and money travel *On facing page:* South when winter comes, searching always for *Sundial on the* more of the sun. Travel agencies supply countless *Council Hall* *at Rapperswil,* folders that feature a sun symbol with bright rays *Switzerland.*

and often a smiling face, inviting one to come where the sun shines warmer.

In many Christian churches people still kneel and lift their faces to a golden sunburst at the altar. We have not, after all, been separated from the sun within ourselves. It is still the bright light without which we could not live, and the pattern of days and nights, of summer and winter, can never be forgotten.

XI. SUN OF IMAGINATION

Sun signs are found in every kind of art and handicraft. Artists have painted the sun in their paintings. Furniture makers have carved sun designs on chairs and chests. Embroiderers have fashioned sun patterns on pillow covers, chair backs, table covers, shirts, and skirts. Weavers have woven the sun into tapestries, beadspreads, shawls, and whatever else they wove. Plates, cups, butter molds, cake forms, clock cases, and many other household items have been decorated with sun designs. Blacksmiths and silversmiths, potters and iron workers, book printers, innkeepers—all these and more have cherished the sun and used its sign somewhere in their work. Often this sun has had a human face.

Paintings on rocks by early people were only the beginning of a long series of sun signs painted or carved on many kinds of surfaces. Designs made by children today are often remarkably like these

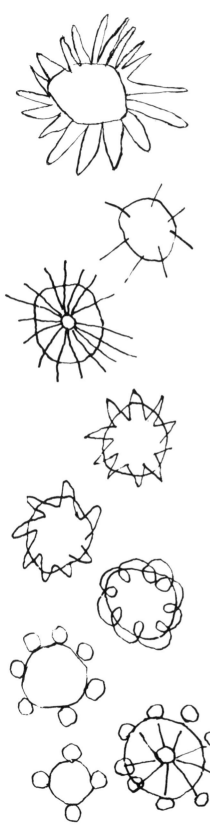

earliest sun signs. They resemble, too, the art of primitive people who are living now. When young children paint or draw they may make sun circles or even sun wheels. They move their whole arm around as they make the circle, feeling its shape. A child will then often paint a cross inside the circle. This is not a picture of the sun; it is a pattern that was already present in the mind of the child, a symbol that is ages old.

These children may live in the United States, in Brazil, in France, in Australia, in Africa—anywhere in the world. Wherever they live, they will make much the same designs, if allowed to paint or draw as they like. In the margin are some typical sun designs made by children.

Of course children do sometimes make pictures of the sun itself. Older children, particularly, make paintings that reflect their experience with the actual sun in the sky. Usually this sun is shown as a source of warmth and joy; often there is a feeling of wonder at our astonishing world.

Sun designs have appealed to artists at every period of history. This vase was made and decorated sometime between 2500 and 1100 B.C., in the Cyclades, a group of Greek islands. The pattern is incised, that is, cut into the surface of the vase. Besides the sun in the center, we have here a

Sun design, paper cutout.
PHOTO BY HARRY HELFMAN.

The sun by a four-year-old French child.
THE SUN IN ART,
THE GRAPHIS PRESS, ZURICH.

THE SUN IN ART, THE GRAPHIS PRESS, ZURICH.

Incised vase from the Cyclades.

spiral variation of the swastika. The fish suggest the ocean on which the sun was thought to journey at night.

The vase with wavy sun rays painted on it was found in the ruins of a king's palace on the island of Crete, in the eastern Mediterranean Sea; it was made about 2000 B.C.

THE SUN IN ART, THE GRAPHIS PRESS, ZURICH.

A third vase, from the island of Cyprus, was painted with a variety of sun disks.

The sun design from a curtain has a pattern in its center that may represent rays, or perhaps the waves of the sea. It was made by Copts, people who belonged to the early Christian church in Egypt, in the fifth century.

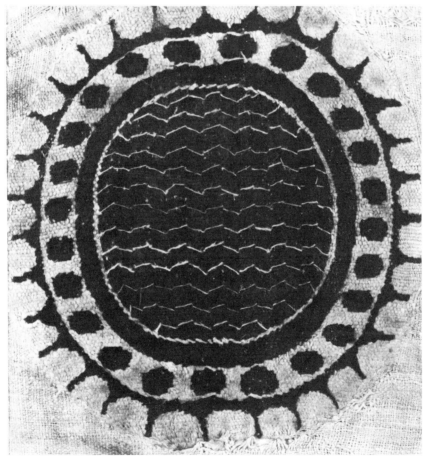

THE SUN IN ART, THE GRAPHIS PRESS, ZURICH.

It was not only artists who were intrigued with sun symbols. In the seventeenth century the French king Louis XIV called the "Sun-King," dressed in a sun costume for a ballet produced in Paris. (A king's crown, in any case, symbolized the sun's rays.)

In about the year 1763 a European innkeeper put up this sign with its painted sun:

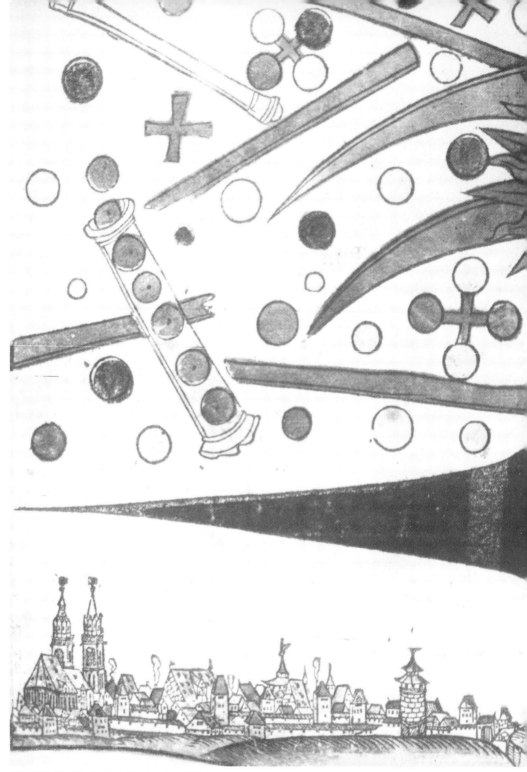

THE SUN IN ART, THE GRAPHIS PRESS, ZURICH.

Before newspapers became widespread, announcements called broadsheets were printed with pictures, songs, or various messages. They were posted on buildings or fences. The broadsheet shown on the previous two pages was made in the sixteenth century from a woodcut. It shows a vision of weird happenings around the sun in the sky.

The principal sun symbol for Christian artists, though they themselves may not always have thought of it that way, was the halo. We have seen an example of this in chapter V. But a great variety of sun designs could be made. The sun often appeared in the stained glass windows of medieval churches and in decorative panels.

Medieval sun design in glass,
made by Glass Masters, New York,
from a fifteenth century panel.

PHOTO BY HARRY HELFMAN.

The Italian Leonardo da Vinci, who lived in the late fifteenth and early sixteenth centuries, was an architect and engineer as well as a painter and sculptor. He made the continuous-line engraving shown above as a symbol of the sun.

Of course not all the artists who portrayed the sun lived in Europe. The Japanese were always fascinated by the sun. A silk scroll painted by the Japanese artist Shibata Zeshin in the nineteenth century is titled *Rising Sun*.

1928 N6 ein Blatt aus dem Städtebuch Klee

The sun did not lose its importance for artists of the twentieth century. *A Leaf from the Book of Towns,* painted by Paul Klee in 1928, shows a bold sun above rows of houses. It is the sun in this picture that seems eternal. Houses are made by man, and they may not last, but the sun is there in the sky forever.

Robert Delaunay's *Sun Disks* is a combination of disks in many colors. One is a huge eye.

MUSEUM
OF MODERN ART,
NEW YORK.

Blast 1, *1957, by Adolph Gottlieb.*

The painting by Adolph Gottlieb is one of a series called "Blast." Each painting in the series has a strong sunlike figure in the upper half of the picture and another abstract design in the lower half.

The sculpture by Richard Lippold is made of gold-filled wire in an abstract pattern of rays that shine like the sun itself.

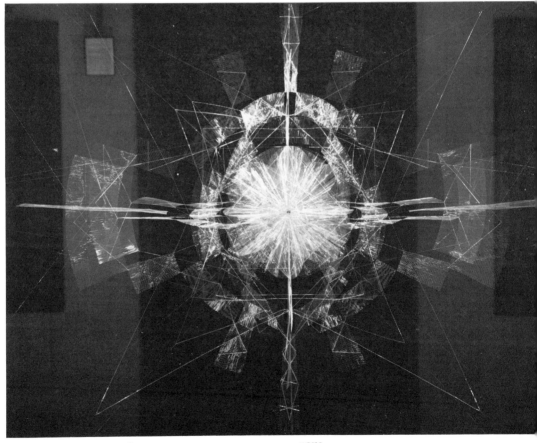

METROPOLITAN MUSEUM OF ART, NEW YORK, FLETCHER FUND, 1956.

Variations Within a Sphere Number 10, The Sun, *by Richard Lippold.*

An Eskimo named Kenojuak, from Cape Dorset in Canada, made a stonecut of the woman in the sun. To the Eskimos, the sun is a beautiful girl pursued by her brother the moon.

Throughout this book we have seen many sun symbols as they appeared on temples, churches, and other public buildings. The modern brick chapel at Massachusetts Institute of Technology uses sun symbolism in still another way. The chapel itself is round, without windows in its walls. It was planned as a quiet retreat, isolated from the distractions of the world outside. Catholics, Protestants, and Jews worship there. The special religious objects used by the different faiths are placed on a marble pedestal at the front of the chapel.

Above the pedestal bright light falls through a round glass window that suggests the sun. At night, electric lights replace the daylight. Behind the pedestal a screen of metal rods hangs from ceiling to floor. Bright metal plates placed across the rods reflect the light from the sun window, bringing it down to earth. They shine like stars.

MASSACHUSETTS INSTITUTE OF TECHNOLOGY

A sun sign can be an emblem used for identification, a kind of trademark. Two Italian printers in the sixteenth century designed the sun at the left as their emblem, or colophon.

Sun signs are very much with us today in trademarks, emblems, and advertising. The colophon of Vintage Books is a sun sign.

A national flag represents not only a country but its purpose, its ideals, and the love people have for that country. There are sun designs on a number of flags in various parts of the world. Japan's, as we have seen, is one big sun. The flag of Nepal has a round sun face and a moon face.

In the center of Argentina's flag is the "Sun of May," in memory of the month in which the country won its freedom from Spain. Uruguay has its own "Sun of May," *El Sol de Mayo.*

The smiling face of the sun greets us on advertising for flights and cruises, vacation clothes, sun-ripened fruits and other foods, even medicines—whatever means vitality and good health. The same bright face often beams on pictures of television sets, sparkling jewelry, bright lamps, kitchen stoves, new laundry soaps—in fact, almost anything. It appears on the wrapping of paper towels, on milk cartons, on matchboxes, and on countless other items. A sun sign is an ages-old symbol that has meaning for everyone, effective in advertising because wherever it appears we are sure to look.

The examples given here of suns used for advertising and as trademarks or emblems are typical. But look around you—you will find many
more.

A sun design seems appropriate, too, for a calendar, made in Japan.

PHOTO BY HARRY HELFMAN.

People today, like those in the past, often choose a sun design when they are hammering an ornament out of tin, making jewelry, embroidering, decorating a bowl, or making a dish.

The square pillow cover in our illustration was embroidered in needlepoint in Spain. A round American pillow has a sun face printed on it. The Mexican tin sun is bright red and makes a charm-

ABOVE: HAMLYN GROUP PICTURE LIBRARY.
BELOW: SOLVEIG COX; PHOTO BY HARRY HELFMAN.

DAWN LEATHER AND BRONZE; PHOTO BY HARRY HELFMAN.

ing wall ornament. An English girl of eight, Elizabeth Elwyn Jones, made the earthenware sun dish
with a smiling face. An American bowl has a
bright sun design in blue inside. A door knocker
of bronze reminds us that the sun is not always

smiling. The tree-fiber mat from Dominica, an island in the West Indies, is a riot of sun circles. (You may remember that *Dominica* is the Latin word for Sunday.)

We have come a long way from early people and their sun wheels drawn on stone. We now know much more about the sun—so much that it is sometimes hard to remember that there is still more, infinitely more, that we do not know. Nothing people have done or believed or learned changes anything about the bright sun in the sky or the turning of the earth or its yearly journey around the sun. The change is in ourselves.

BOOKS FOR FURTHER READING

ADULT BOOKS

Corti, Walter Robert, THE SUN.
NEW YORK: BOBBS-MERRILL, ODYSSEY PRESS, 1964.

Gelling, Peter, and Hilda Ellis Davidson,
THE CHARIOT OF THE SUN.
LONDON: J. M. DENT AND SONS, 1969.

Hawkes, Jacquetta, MAN AND THE SUN.
NEW YORK: RANDOM HOUSE, 1962.

Herdeg, Walter, ed., THE SUN IN ART.
ZURICH: THE GRAPHIS PRESS, 1962.

Lalou, Étienne, THE ORION BOOK OF THE SUN.
NEW YORK: GROSSMAN PUBLISHERS, ORION PRESS, 1960.

NEW LAROUSSE ENCYCLOPEDIA OF MYTHOLOGY.
LONDON: PROMETHEUS PRESS, 1968.

BOOKS FOR CHILDREN

Asimov, Isaac, THE KINGDOM OF THE SUN.
NEW YORK: ABELARD SCHUMAN, 1963.

Gallant, Roy A., EXPLORING THE SUN.
GARDEN CITY: DOUBLEDAY, 1958.

Helfman, Elizabeth S.,
SIGNS AND SYMBOLS AROUND THE WORLD.
NEW YORK: LOTHROP, LEE & SHEPARD, 1967.

————, CELEBRATING NATURE.
NEW YORK: THE SEABURY PRESS, 1969.

Hey, Nigel, THE MYSTERIOUS SUN.
NEW YORK: G. P. PUTNAM'S SONS, 1971.

Knight, David C., THE FIRST BOOK OF THE SUN.
NEW YORK: FRANKLIN WATTS, 1968.

Marshall, Roy K., SUNDIALS.
NEW YORK: MACMILLAN, 1963.

Zim, Herbert S., THE SUN.
NEW YORK: WILLIAM MORROW, 1953.

INDEX

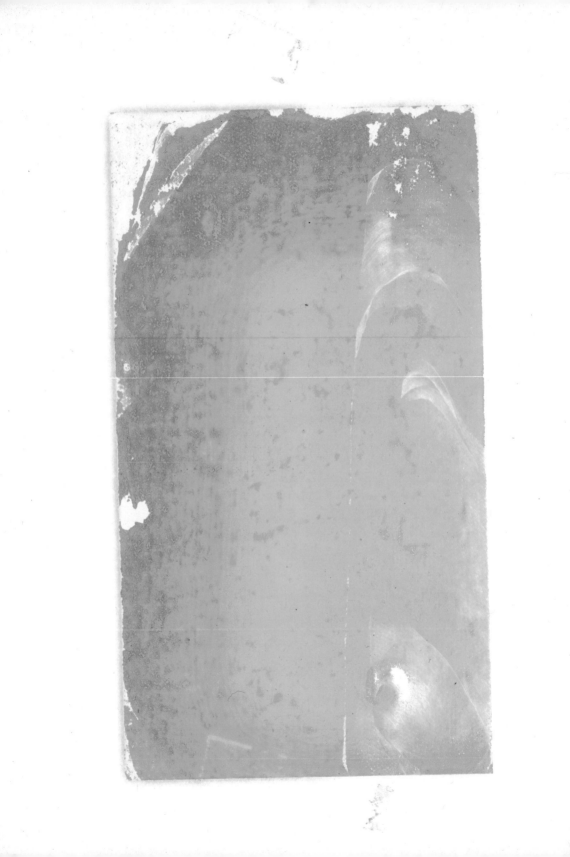